Before the Call

The Communication Playbook

Before the Call

The Communication Playbook

By Dr. Roderick J. Bartell, R.O.D.C.

ISBN 978-1-58776-924-5
Nonfiction; Business
Library of Congress catalog card number: 2011944403

Manufactured in the United States of America
NetPublications, Inc

675 Dutchess Turnpike, Poughkeepsie, NY 12603
www.hudsonhousepub.com (800) 724-1100

Acknowledgments

It is true you can't do it all alone. I found it especially true in writing this book. I thank Kathy, my wife for her total support and excellent ideas; Nikki Williams who edited each chapter, was my technical writing assistant and publishing coordinator; my mother Mary Bartell, who proofed the text – at age 96.

I would like to thank the team at Bartell & Bartell, Ltd. for giving me the time to write. Lastly, I want to thank Verne Harnish, author of "Mastering the Rockefeller Habits," for his excellent and helpful suggestions.

Special Thanks to those Alumni of the 100th Leadership Flight School who shared their comments with us.

June 20 – 24, 2011

"MVP is an excellent tool to improve the quality of all of your communications, and will help ensure you 'get it right' on those especially difficult ones. The MVP tool is one anyone can use and that leaders will want to keep with them at all times."

Tony Baker
Director of Program Management
ArtiFlex Manufacturing, LLC

"The servant leadership model has tremendous heart and gives hope for better human interaction. Shawn [Ishler], Bill [Brashers] and Rod [Bartell] provide brilliant insights into human behavior that can be applied to business practice. Use of diagnostic profiles are internalized by them so thoroughly that they are able to provide specific, tangible information for workplace solutions and teach others to approach their workplace in the same way. Thanks guys!"

Kim Banister
Education Specialist/Gallery Curator
Harrisburg Area Community College

"MVP is life altering both personally and professionally. It will change your interactions with your co-workers, clients, supervisors, parents, children, spouse, and friends. Just try it... and keep trying..."

Cheryl Bartram
Director of Wealth Administration
Abundance Wealth Counselors

"MVP has the ability to transform my communication with my boss, co-workers, employees, family and friends. The genius is in its simplicity – viewing the one I am communicating with as an 'MVP' ensures my motivation, vision and paradigm is helpful."

Adam Chenevey
Operations Manager
ArtiFlex Manufacturing, LLC

"MVP is one of the most powerful tools you will ever need as a leader. I can't wait to return to work and practice unleashing the 'new me'."

Steve Giauque
Manufacturing Manager
ArtiFlex Manufacturing, LLC

"Reminding yourself, as often as necessary, to apply MVP in a positive light will change your Paradigm from a variable negative lens to a very positive lens. MVP is not a painful approach; MVP is a comforting approach. MVP generates a buoyant feeling."

Charlotte Layton
Quality Manager
American Refining Group, Inc.

"This has been the most enlightening and enriching program I have ever attended. I find that these principles not only can be applied to my professional development but also for my personal development. I can't wait to begin my new transition."

Lisa Stanton
Logistics Manager
Spartanburg Steel Products

"For me, Rod Bartell and his Team have just started me down a correct path in life."

Fred Stauffer
Process Supervisor
American Refining Group, Inc.

"MVP is a great tool to use in any situation! The time invested in preparing an MVP pays off many times over."

Matt Steele
Director – Systems, Quality and Purchasing
ArtiFlex Manufacturing, LLC

"MVP is a powerful tool to use in communication. It sets the stage for positive interaction even under difficult circumstances, and anyone can use it effectively."

Linda Taylor
Controller
Scotland Manufacturing, Inc.

Table of Contents

Forward

For years, clients have asked, "why don't you write a book about what you do?" The answer did not come easy – it wasn't for lack of subject matter, but which topic would be most interesting. Should it be a textbook, a well-masked compilation of interesting client anecdotes or a "how to" book?

After considerable thought and discussion with peers and close friends, it became apparent where to start my writing. In working with a wide range of corporate executives and other clients, when asked, "where does it hurt?" the same answer surfaces – "it is a communication problem." A variation on this theme is, "we're having a personality conflict," but when probed deeper the client reveals a "communication problem."

Having spent many years studying, diagnosing and intervening with complex organizations, the similarities between these organizations and the human body are striking. Whether the work group or organization is a police department, school, hospital or a Fortune 500 company, communication is the lifeblood, or circulatory system. Poor communication will have the same impact as a partial arterial blockage – the affected organ can become damaged and inoperative. Good communication is a key element of healthy relationships. Healthy relationships allow trust to form; trust is the foundation on which we build high performing teams and organizations.

Therefore, writing a book on how to obtain quality communications seemed a useful and logical starting place. "Before the Call" is for those who have a desire for a mastery of communications, better relationships and a healthier workplace. It simply provides a template to achieve success in these areas. May this book assist you toward that end.

It is designed to be an easy read, something that can be read in one plane trip across the continent, replace a boring television program or complement your early morning coffee – even serve as an interesting read for a neighborhood book club. Enjoy!

1
The Power of MVP

You're hard at work in your cubicle, it's not much but it's a desk to call your own – you earned it the old-fashioned way, you worked for it. Lately, your work is piling up around you – probably because you're wearing too many hats. A page from the executive assistant, "Mr. Bigdome is on line 2..." interrupts you. You can hear your boss yelling obscenities in the background. Slowly, you reach for the phone...

As you pull out into the intersection, a car speeds up behind you and continues to follow too closely for several blocks despite your slowing down for him to pass you. As you approach a red light, you carefully slow to a stop, keeping an eye in your rearview mirror on the tailgating vehicle. Suddenly you are jolted forward by the car behind you. You stop the car and open the door...

Your teenager has been begging to take the car out on Friday night, and doesn't seem to take "no" for an answer. You're about to make it clear for the last time...

This is the part of being a police officer and public servant you hate the most – delivering bad news. It was no one's fault, just a dark night, wet roads, a bad curve, and a bad accident. You reach for the doorbell…

It's a big deal and you are leading the team making a presentation to a potential investor for your company. It's been a long time coming; it could finally be payday. With laser pointer in hand, you begin…

Nervous, yes. You really need a job and this one seems perfect. Within an easy commute, reasonable money and full benefits. They just called your name, all eyes in the reception area seem to be looking at you as you stand and proceed toward the conference room…

You can't put off answering this email any longer. You don't really know how to say no but the last four nights have been sleepless as you examine the ramifications of a "yes" response. With emotion, your fingertips touch the keys…

There is that dog again. A new neighbor with three small kids is one thing but a new puppy too? It is just too much. What a way to welcome your neighbor. You set your jaw as you enter their backyard to lay down the law...

Eight challenging situations. The one thing in common? The use of MVP will greatly enhance the probability of a successful outcome in every case. Used properly, MVP transforms a potentially negative event into a positive result. Simply stated, MVP is the positive mental power tool to help you achieve mastery in your communications, whether it is an email, a phone call, a face-to-face conversation or a group presentation. It is true that good communications establish successful relationships –MVP plays the center role with a positive Motivation, Vision and Paradigm.

The MVP acronym represents the three components that make up the formula to achieve this communication mastery: a positive mix of Motivation, Vision and Paradigm. It works when you are under pressure, upset, frustrated, or even challenged. Done properly, it will improve every communication encounter – so you won't ever need to ask yourself, "is now the time to use it?"

MVP is a positive mix of **M**otivation, **V**ision and **P**aradigm.

MVP is quick to learn, easy-to-use and effective in any communication involving two or more people, regardless of your experience with the person. The key – do not start a conversation, any conversation, until your MVP is in place.

MVP is a tool to enhance communications, making them consistently more efficient and constructive, not something to spice up a dialog or to act as a conversation filler to give you time to think of something clever to say. MVP is the tool that will predictably enhance any and every communication you have, regardless of topic. It's a template!

The first introduction of MVP was in 2002 to executives participating in a weeklong leadership course created by Bartell & Bartell, Ltd. known as Leadership Flight School™. Over the years and many Leadership Flight Schools later, hundreds of executives around the world have successfully documented the power of MVP. During the course's graduation ceremony, each executive shares what one topic or concept got their attention the most and will be helpful in the workplace for daily use. Over 50% of the responses from all graduations cited MVP. Old and new graduates alike continue to use MVP – approximately 85% of alumni surveyed apply MVP on a regular basis.

MVP sets the positive tone needed for successful communication. Sometimes the words we use are awkward or imprecise. Have you ever said to yourself, "I wish I had said…" after a conversation? However, it is the intent or tone of the conversation that will bleed through the actual words and subtly communicate to the listener what the real message is behind the message. The listener will be able to determine the real intent of the message, be it positive or negative, even if the words don't clearly express this message.

Do not start a conversation - any conversation - until your MVP is in place.

Nonverbal communication, often referred to as "body language," is a true form of communication. MVP is important for this communication as well. According to team-building specialists, everyone in a room communicates equally during a team discussion. Some are more verbal and others are more nonverbal, but communicating just the same. Therefore, MVP is critical in preparing for a team session even if active verbal conversation is not one's choice. In nonverbal communication, it takes very little for the receiver of the message to pick up the tone and intensity of the communication. The "message" bleeds through the silence. If the receiver is a dominant "S" temperament (as we'll discuss later), there becomes a true free flow of information. A roll of the eyes, the folding of the arms, a sudden shift or posture can also miscommunicate the desired message. Using MVP, nonverbal miscommunication decreases and the experience for all team participants becomes more efficient and comfortable. The message does not become lost.

Use MVP to prepare for nonverbal communication as well as verbal.

Think of the number of thoughts that can be communicated with a non-word like, "uh huh." Depending on the inflection of the voice, it can mean agreement, disagreement, thoughtful reflection, surprise, or even rejection. MVP ensures this tone, or "background" message aligns with and reinforces the verbal part of the message.

MVP acts to sort out and organize your thoughts prior to communicating. It will allow you to deliver a clear, positive message – even under pressure. It increases the probability that the message will be received as best as possible regardless of the topic.

MVP keeps you on your purpose even when the tension is high, others are deflecting your efforts to communicate or the complexity of your message makes it difficult to deliver. It keeps you focused when the communication could be emotionally upsetting to all involved.

Simply, MVP becomes a "best practice" for any communicator, using any medium, for any purpose.

In its basic form, MVP is easier to learn than driving a car or using a cell phone. The first step is to ask two questions:

1) Do I want my conversations to be effective and/or respected by others; and,

2) Do I want to improve my relationships with others?

If you do, go on reading and enjoy!

Many ask, "OK, how long does it take? I'm an urgent, bottom line, Type-A personality." Typically, it takes a minute or less to set up a MVP. Regular users report it takes no more time than from the moment it takes to be told, "Mr. Jones is on line three," to the time you pick up the call. More importantly, MVP use is cumulative; the more you use it, the more efficient and effective the communications become – which in reality saves time and aggravation. The more you practice and use it, the less time it will take to use MVP effectively.

However, as a consistent user of MVP, I have found that the more adversarial the situation, the longer it will take to develop a workable motivation, vision and paradigm. One client intervention stands out as a clear example. Although I have had the opportunity to work with numerous partner conflicts in business settings, this one was very contentious.

> The more adversarial the situation, the longer it will take to develop a workable MVP.

It was a husband and wife business partnership, each of a different cultural and educational background. The business had grown successfully over 16 years but the constant quarreling between these individuals had a severe impact. The president, the husband, was very dictatorial and disrespectful in his speech towards his wife, his business partner. The wife was the technical driver that truly made the business competitive.

She had grown tired of her mistreatment. He could not see his behavior as an issue, and requested an intervention to "set her straight." He even suggested he would bring his attorney along in case the intervention "went south". It literally took me three weeks to generate a positive MVP about this intervention. After re-contracting with both parties, I was able to generate a workable MVP, and the problem was resolved.

Those who are not natural conversationalists or who tend to be a bit reticent or shy, ask, "Is this even possible for me to use?" The answer is yes, without a doubt! Based on my experience working with shy, introverted people, I find they actually are more precise in applying the MVP approach and obtain excellent results.

Others, very sensitive to culture, race and religion ask, "Does MVP, in any way, violate or disrespect the person with whom you are communicating?" No. Instead, it acts to reduce the tension and potential misunderstandings that can occur from clumsy communications.

MVP is a pre-communication or communication preparation process. This process is actually a template that guides your pre-communication formulation effort and keeps helping you during the delivery of the message. This template, properly used, will unleash the communication skills you already possess towards your objective. It will not come naturally to anyone; it must be learned. Some individuals will find it easier to learn but with a reasonable amount of practice, anyone can effectively master this technique. Without question, your communication will improve significantly even with a loose adherence to this template.

MVP does require some self-discipline until it becomes habitual. However, the more you focus, the better your experience will be and the more you'll enjoy predictable results.

By its nature, MVP enhances the value of communication and telegraphs to the other person a feeling that he or she is important.

Skeptics, rightfully, ask whether this template has been tested. As previously mentioned, over the last several years *Bartell & Bartell, Ltd.* has been conducting an advanced leadership school – called Leadership Flight School™ for supervisors, managers, technical professionals and senior executives. When formally surveyed, 85% of attendees reported that one of the most important tools they consistently use and value is MVP, with only the general concept of servant leadership scoring higher.

Sustainability was also measured and 70% of the alumni that attended from the period of 2002-2006 indicated they still were using MVP. From the 2007 to the present, 88% of alumni indicated they were using MVP. Reportedly MVP contributed to the mending of several marriages, reversing career slides and enhancing relationships and lives overall.

MVP is more powerful and useful than a pre-written script because it is flexible. Regardless of the other person's reply, you will be able to formulate a response that is positive and will consistently move your message forward in a manner that your listener can effectively receive. Therefore, MVP helps the receiver as well as the sender of the message. MVP provides the intended receiver with a clear understanding of the intent of the message. The receiver automatically does this by:

1. Selecting a paradigm, or lens, that is most helpful, accurate and efficient in "decoding" the message into understanding; and,
2. Discerning the tone and body language used to convey the message.

The message can then be understood as intended – both verbally and non-verbally.

The power of MVP is not just in helping you send the message, but in helping the receiver understand the message as it was truly intended – even if awkward, crude or incomplete when transmitted.

For example, compare the following two emails – one using MVP and one without.

Efficient email from Superior to Subordinate without MVP:

Sorry I missed your presentation. I've been having a hectic life what with budget cuts and all. I guess we all have to keep swinging at the ball and hope we hit some. Keep swinging.
--Ralph

MVP-driven email from the same superior to the same subordinate:

Linda,
You once again came through for our team – I heard you represented us well. Thank you.
For my part, I sincerely apologize for not letting you know ahead of time that I could not be there. However, it feels great knowing our flag is being carried under even the most difficult of times. Our future is bright with you on our team.
--Ralph

Are there levels of MVP skill? Absolutely. The more you practice, the better you will become.

2

An Introduction to the MVP Elements

For a technique to work under all conditions, regardless of the pressure or emotions of the moment, it must be straightforward. MVP meets this "Keep it Simple" process. The elements are Motivation, Vision, and Paradigm.

Motivation is what you want to achieve with the communication. Vision is your anticipated outcome of this specific communication event. Paradigm is the lens that you choose to look through during this communication. When all three are clear and positive, you are ready for your communications. Sounds simple, right? Let's take a look at Bob's MVP in action.

During his presentation, Bob glanced at the clock on the wall, then around the room at his team. He was missing one member; Percy was late again. This meeting was very important and Percy needed to participate in the planning process. As the 8 o'clock meeting wrapped up, Percy walked right past the doorway and headed to his own office. *This is the third time in two weeks*, thought Bob. *I've already spoken with him twice and he just muttered some weak excuses both times.* Bob scratched his head of thinning hair. *I'm done with this disrespect toward me and my meetings*, he continued as he picked up the pace toward Percy's office. *He is being paid well, why doesn't he get it? He's my IT guru and I need him, but this is just too much.*

By the time Bob reached Percy's office, he was substantially irritated. "Percy, I want to see you in my office," he ordered, "we need to talk – now." Pivoting on his heels, Bob turned back through the maze of cubicles and forced his heavy, corner office door open. Percy entered just a few steps behind him.

"Percy, what is your problem?" Bob asked, standing by his desk rather than sitting in his leather chair. Percy sat down in the guest chair across the room, staring at Bob coldly through dark-circled eyes. "Well?"

Percy shifted his weight in the chair and looked at Bob. "What do you want from me?" responded Percy, finally. "Just give me the notes from the meeting… if there are any," he muttered.

"That's it!" said Bob as he slapped his desk. *What Percy really needs is an attitude adjustment, but my schedule is just too full today*, he thought. "Percy, tomorrow at 0800 sharp we'll meet and get this straightened out." *Milita* *seemed to set a more serious tone in tough co* thought. Bob stood still, fuming.

Percy sighed. He shook his head, l window at the threatening clouds outside, and then turned toward the door without another word.

Alone, Bob continued to mull over his problem with Percy. *He's probably too far gone to be of any use to the team, maybe the shipping department could use him – they run a loose ship*, thought Bob. *Too bad, though. Percy was a talented systems designer.*

Shuffling through papers and sticky notes, Bob came across a book he hadn't noticed before. "Before the Call," he read aloud, "The Communication Playbook." With the wife and kids at his in-laws for the week, he'd have some time to read it tonight. *Could be helpful*, he thought.

The next morning at 7:30, Bob decided to put this MVP thing to work. *It said you have to have a positive motivation, a positive vision and a positive paradigm*, he thought, *before you start any conversation.*

Bob's motivation had been to get Percy's attention and discipline him so he won't mess with the team again. *I guess that's not very positive*, he thought. Bob considered it for a ent. Percy should want to join the team instead of distancing himself from it. *I'd say that's positive,* Bob smiled. *All right, now to vision the outcome of the meeting. He probably won't even be on time.* Bob began to pace. *But what if the outcome is that Percy feels this conversation was constructive and informative, worth his time and that he looks forward to our next conversation? I'd really like for that kind of connection to form.*

Feeling more positive about the upcoming meeting, Bob paused to think about the third element of MVP. His original paradigm was negative, that Percy was a "bad boy," a "rebel," and "out of control." *That's a dark lens to see a person through. Percy is talented, and he did produce smart ideas and represented our team well when other teams met with us. I guess I could adjust my paradigm to see him as a valued member of the team*, he thought, *someone worth keeping*. Bob continued to focus on his new positive MVP as he prepared for the meeting. Feeling as though a small weight had been lifted, Bob realized he didn't feel the same way about this situation as he had yesterday. *Maybe there is something to this MVP stuff.*

At 8 o'clock sharp, Percy appeared in Bob's doorway with two coffees in hand.

Nice peace offering, Bob thought. *Oops, I slipped back into a negative MVP*. Bob accepted the coffee and smiled at Percy, stepping aside to allow him through the door.

"Thank you, Percy," Bob said, "come in and make yourself at home." With Percy's back to him, Bob quickly shook his head in surprise. *Did I really just say that*? He took a sip of the bitter coffee and composed his thought.

Bob leaned against the front of his desk and set the coffee down. "Percy, I want to discuss with you how important you are to this team and how we need to better connect with your talents," Bob said, feeling confident about his opening. "You work hard and contribute a lot, but how can we tap your valuable input when we meet?"

Before Bob continued, Percy interjected. "I didn't mean to miss the morning meeting yesterday. I had worked until 5:30 yesterday morning on the Q-Team project and was just going to go home to shower and then be right back," Percy rubbed his eyes, "I laid down for just a minute, but when I woke up it was already 8:15. Just great! It was my third all-nighter in three weeks, and I know I let you down before," Percy paused for a moment to take a sip of his steaming coffee. With a sigh, he added, "I guess I'm just not as young as I used to be."

Bob's eyes had widened as Percy spoke, and his mouth hung open slightly. "I knew you were working hard and making progress in untangling the Q-Team mess, but honestly, you've been pulling all-nighters?" The corner of Bob's mouth twitched upward into a smile of realization. "Thank you."

The two men stare at each other for a moment, both feeling relieved. "I think we need to talk more," Bob finally said, "the ball is in my court to make the time for you, Percy."

Percy nodded, leaned forward and offered, "Would it be helpful if I presented a brief summary to the team on the process I've been using to untangle the Q-Team spaghetti mess? Maybe they could help me think about how we can avoid the same mistake from happening in the future."

"That sounds great," Bob responded, "allow me to introduce your presentation. Sometimes we feel our good work speaks for us, but it often takes a team to recognize it – let me help you." Percy accepted and extended his right hand, which Bob shook enthusiastically. He watched Percy leave and reflected on his approach to MVP. *My paradigm was right, he is worth keeping. I think we'll enjoy future sessions.* He picked up the coffee and held it to his lips. *It's great to be the boss.*

Your MVP must be positive before it can be effective.

How often do we find that we're wrong about someone, their value or motivations? Even worse, how often do we go on not knowing how wrong we were? Others move on with their lives and we never recognize that our paradigm about them was wrong. It's not unlike two ships passing in the night when a valuable connection is never realized. MVP gives us a chance to make that valuable connection.

MVP does make whomever we're communicating with a Most Valuable Player created by our positive Motivation, Vision and Paradigm.

Using MVP makes the target of our efforts a Most Valuable Player.

Do not dismiss "MVP" as nothing more than keeping positive. For MVP to work you must be positive – but in all three of the components – Motivation, Vision and Paradigm. A negative MVP can destroy relationships and create conflict. It is most noticeable with people you have authority over, such as family (especially your children), or those you supervise.

Organizations, from businesses to government, can become "sick" or dysfunctional for many reasons. Often there are a number of factors that, when taken together, become the cause for an organization's problem. The coping processes that the organizational members use to address these harmful, cause-effect factors are often classified as an organizational syndrome. Although not necessarily intentional, dysfunctional organizational coping mechanisms or syndromes take place in many forms. Let's examine one such syndrome. A deadly organizational syndrome to an organization is the Management Rejection Syndrome, or MGT Syndrome. The members of a work/organizational unit reject or "fire" their supervisor. Although subordinates don't have the authority to terminate the boss, they can, and do, stop following. As a result, the supervisor can no longer play the role of leader, regardless of what top management decrees. The supervisor typically triggers this MGT syndrome, often unknowingly, using a negative MVP.

A leader must have one specific ingredient to be a leader: followers. An individual has the power to choose to follow or make you their leader. You can desire it, wish it, ask for it, but you can't demand that they follow you. A positive MVP is one of the greatest tools to obtain a position of leadership and retain it. The opposite of being a leader is not a follower, but becoming a victim. A negative MVP can set up such a dynamic.

A positive MVP is one of the greatest tools to obtain a position of leadership and retain it.

It is common for an organization's dysfunction to be labeled as a "communication problem." This is too broad of a diagnosis to be helpful. When examined more carefully, a negative MVP is often at the center of this "communication problem."

MVP, although subtle to the casual observer, is a powerful tool when used. It changes the dynamics and effectiveness of any communication event. It directly affects leadership, relationships, your organization's health, and more!

3

The Three Legged Stool

So, what is the impact of MVP if members of an organization use it consistently? Without question, it has a direct and very significant effect on the individuals using MVP and their relationships. The communication patterns and relationships grow stronger each time they exercise it. It bonds people together, increases understanding, decreases conflict, and makes our lives all around more pleasant. But what about the impact on the organizations that are inhabited by consistent practioners of MVP? The key word is, "consistent."

Intermittent use of MVP is of value as it pulses a boost of positive energy throughout the organization where it's used. In a low-level way, the organization is positively conditioned and sensitized to receive another MVP experience. The MVP dynamic, being a pre-communication process, is only experienced or measurable from improved outputs of relationships built by the better communications. The dynamic would look as follows:

Organization Development Chain

Organization Increases to "Fitness" Level

↑

Organizational Purpose Achieved

↑

Greater Organizational Efficiency/Effectiveness

↑

Increased Organizational Health

↑

Stronger Relationships
(less negative coping mechanisms/syndromes)

↑

Improved Communication
(regardless of communication method used)

↑

Positive MVP
(consistently used)

MVP, by its nature, is hidden from view but its influence on an organization can be great. In fact, the three MVP elements – Motivation, Vision, and Paradigm – act as the three legs of a stool on which is the organization's architecture and the organization's "fitness" ultimately achieved.

Communication, the circulation of the informational life-blood of any organization, becomes the seat of the stool. This provides the organizational architecture with a strong, predictable base. The core of this architecture consists of five components.

Organizational Architecture Elements:

- Leadership – guides and monitors the continuous development of the organization.
- Structure – how the human resources are selected, developed and assembled into work teams and functions.
- Culture – the values, standards, ethics and work environment that encourages excellent performance.
- Process – the work logic and flow that optimizes resource applications.
- IC Δ OI – the transformation of the Intellectual Capital (IC) residing within the organization's members (their expertise, experience, and education) into Organizational Intelligence (OI) which generates the vision, creativity, strategy and tactics necessary for developing a competitive edge, success and long term survival.

Let's explore the role MVP plays in this organizational architectural process. Before we discuss leadership, we must clarify the difference between management and leadership and, for that matter, the difference between charisma and leadership.

Without this clarification, the MVP discussion and application is thin at best when placed into organizational context.

Managerial history has evolved the need for MVP. Let's go back to World War II. The United States of America marshaled its human resources and in a few short months turned farm kids and city kids alike into effective soldiers. These young men and women were capable of dealing with the challenges of war and many of them returned home to enter the civilian work force. Their training, tough as it was, got them through the war experience. Their drill instructors were, in many cases, their first real managers. Time was of the essence and the model was simple and effective. As the one-way arrow depicts, "You do what I say," (diagrammed below).

Drill Instructor

Soldier

These young people matured into our supervisors, managers and executives of the 1960's. However, their employees, the baby boomer generation, were just entering the work force. The boomers felt comfortable challenging the status quo, they dreamed of a better work world and were not above taking on the "establishment." By the end of the 1960's, they were demanding an increased say in their management.

With help from the unions, especially in local government, the management had to shift again. This time the arrows of communication were forced to go both ways as shown below.

For the first time, communication became important to the complex, evolving organization, although in a rather simple form. The manager style of communications was typically the "parent," and largely expected the employee to respond as the "child," if they were to get along and progress.

This parent-child mode of communication was not well received. Academia went to work to develop a more acceptable model. Ten years passed and the "participative manager" model rolled out as the "better way." Although developed in the early 60's, it was only widely adopted some 20 years later. Diagrammatically it looked as follows:

Rank was removed when appropriate and a free flow of communication was established. However, the manager's role stayed relatively the same as in the second model, except now manager was now stylistically more gentle and kind. Some practioners disparagingly labeled it "touchy feely."

Problems with the model started to surface with questions like, "How close should I get to my employees if I am their friend? How can I go back and discipline them?" This put the manager into a boss-buddy bind. The result was the breakdown of trust, which is truly the foundation of any effective organization. Therefore, the model was largely set aside or discarded.

Another decade passed and the search was on for a better manager model – one that took into consideration the introduction of fast-developing, complex, technically focused companies that now had to compete in the ever-changing world marketplace. Employees were well educated and starting to see the business organization as their life investment of choice. No longer did a company hire an employee just to meet their corporate needs. It had to meet the needs of the employee. The employee's talent, experience, value and contribution was now portable. The employee was now making employment decisions more short term about where he or she could receive the best return on investment for his or her education, expertise and experience that he or she was offering to the employer. Along with this shift in paradigm about the work place was the employee's desire to be treated as a valued contributor at his or her place of work. The servant-leader model was reborn, resurrected from history some 2,000 years ago.

The servant-leader model has all the qualities that meet all the new work contributor's desires and hopes. The model is illustrated below.

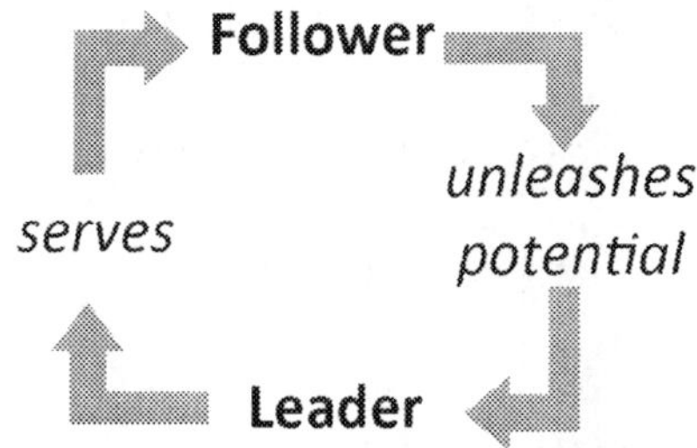

The manager must now shift to become a leader. In all three of the previous models, the manager held the control, responsibility, status and authority by the hiring organization. The manager held his or her position as long as the senior management approved it. Management was based in power and control. With servant leadership, leaders require one special quality – they need followers. Seemingly trite, it is a significant difference. The servant leader must be able to consistently determine and access the "What's In It For Me," or "WIIFM" for each of his or her personnel, whether they're called subordinates, employees, followers, peers, partners, associates, etc. This servant leader obtains and holds the title of leader only if the work team awards it to him or her. The employees cannot be compelled to follow and can withdraw the servant leader position from their "supervisor" whenever they choose. Simply stated, managers control and leaders serve. Ah, can you now see the vital role of a positive motivation, vision and paradigm?

Managers control and leaders serve.

Under the servant-leader model, communication ceases to be parent-to-child and becomes adult-to-adult. MVP makes this possible. In addition to the communication shift, there is the needed shift by the employee from being externally motivated, developed, managed, coordinated, rewarded, etc., to becoming internally or self motivated, developed, managed, coordinated, rewarded, etc. A new level of personal maturity is now required for the servant-leader model to work most effectively. This maturity is easily discerned as the individual becomes OTHER centric – the underlying foundation of MVP.

The challenge to current organizations is huge. The shift is shown in the following diagram.

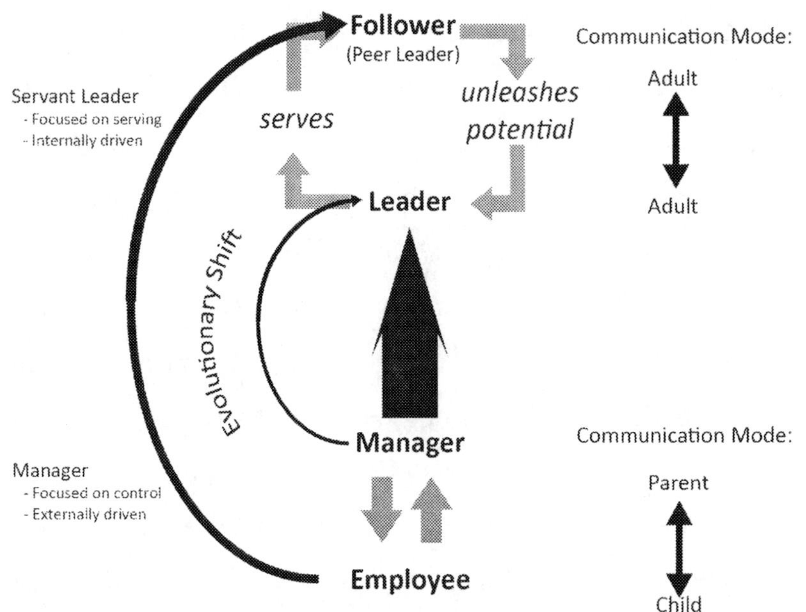

Organizational Architecture: Leadership

In the servant-leadership model, the focus shifts from control to serving the employee, from externally driven to internally motivated, from parent-to-child to an adult-to-adult mode of communications.

This shift from manager to leader and employee to follower or peer leader (as shown by the large arrows above) is not only significant but also challenging to accomplish. Employees not only have to be selected for the internally driven attribute but for their desire to develop into a mature adult-to-adult communicator. Having assessed thousands of managers and executives the last forty or so years, it is easier to select for the qualities than try to develop them quickly. Managers must not only develop the basic managerial skills but also be able to apply them with a servant-leader approach. Leaders going through this shift will find legacy employees trying to drag their new leader back into their former manager mode. In the former management mode it was easier – for the employee to be told what to do ("externally" managed) and having the luxury of critiquing the boss at will, as part of the old parent-to-child communications culture. With the enlightened servant leader model, the employee has as much accountability as their leader. There is no place for pushing the blame up to the boss. On the other hand, the employee is no longer constrained by the manager. In the past, no one would dare to go beyond, challenge, or compete with the boss without a subtle or not-so-subtle course of disciplinary action. The new servant leader would recognize the need to develop his or her team effectively through improved communications and mentoring. This is the key to a successful future for the organization.

Another core attribute of this new servant leadership model is the ability to communicate, and communicate well. As previously mentioned, it is the platform for developing an effective organization. However, charisma alone is not enough of a leader quality to attract the employee of this era. It is someone who cares about them, their development, their success and their future who will win their followership. Under this new model of servant leadership, the leader of the future will need to be excellent in communications when he or she speaks. Words will be magnified throughout the organization and the slight slip-ups of the past will become full-blown mistakes known by all in the organization in the future.

What people want in a leader has been researched extensively but being able to connect, establish trust, communicate and develop a meaningful relationship is the golden thread that weaves throughout these core dimensions. Again, MVP is the method that makes this predictability possible.

Organizational Architecture: Structure

Structure is a lot more than organizational charts, power charts, chain of command, span of control, and governance. More importantly is the building and unleashing of work teams and minimization of organizational silos or excessive boundary intensity between work groups. It only starts with formal charting. The formation of synergistic teams powerfully drives a company to meet goals and move strategically to reach a vision of the future. The leader's focus unleashes the excellence of these teams. The traditional model was for the manager to focus primarily on the task while keeping the team motivated (driven) towards the task. The evolving servant leader model focuses on the team and encourages, through leadership, the team to focus on the task. The servant leader monitors the task progress to provide feedback as to how to lead the team to optimal health and effectiveness. This dynamic is a significant paradigm shift and is depicted below:

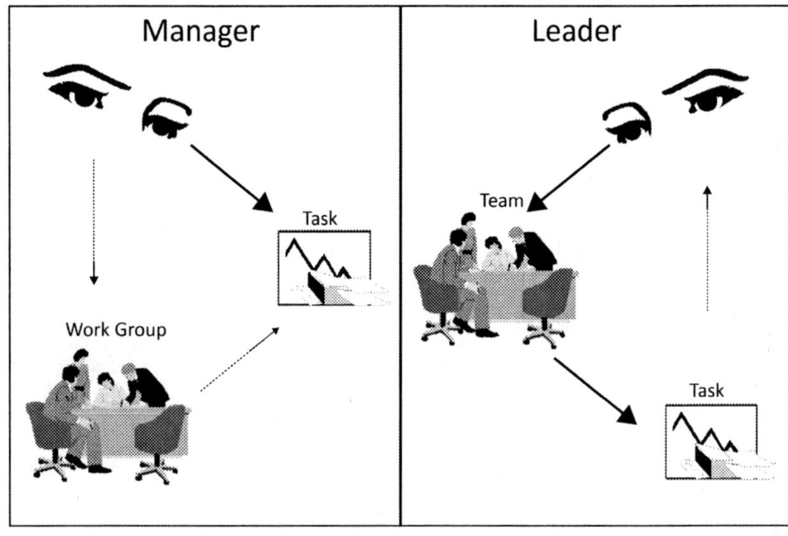

This new kind of team health is founded on trust and communication. MVP is the tool that everyone can use – regardless of the level of team experience, responsibility or accountability. All members of the team benefit from the positive use of this skill.

Organizational Architecture: Culture

Culture, the third component of organizational architecture, is defined in the organizational world by communication behaviors – their styles, processes, ability to interpret and translate history accurately and bring it forward, relationship bonds or connections, ethics and value agreements. Poor communications negatively influences organizational cultures by keeping critical bonding from occurring that is necessary for cultures to be maintained, reinforced and embraced. Without communication reinforcement, the generation of constructive cultures can't occur and organizations slowly degenerate and become victims of entropy. The Organization Utility Index (OUI), developed by the Institute of Organizational Science exemplifies this entropic dynamic. It directly translates to MVP and communication. The OUI is an organizational measurement of the range from entropy to synergy. It reports how efficiently the resources are used or how much "horsepower" is getting to the wheels of the business or work unit. As shown below, the range of OUI goes from -100 to 200.

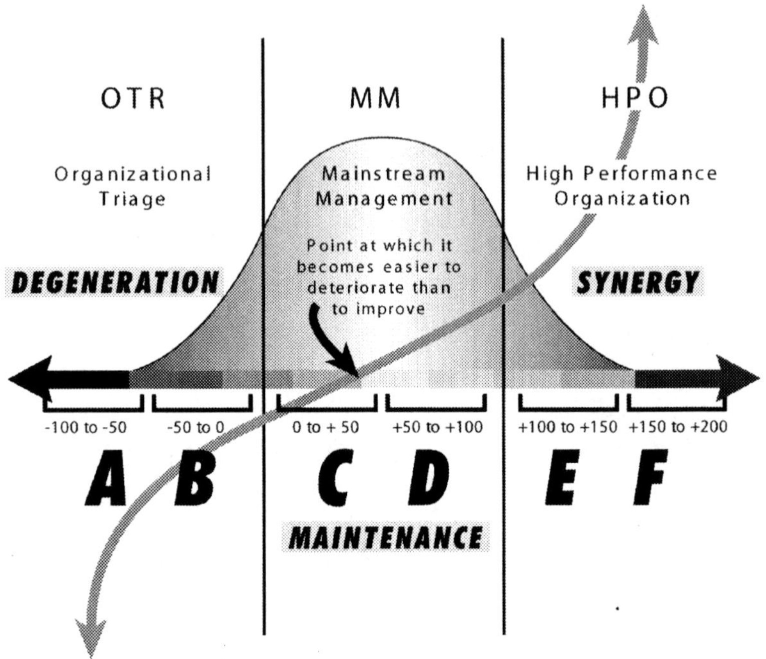

The normal range is 0 to 100. Change occurs linearly in this normal range. At the extremes (-100 to 0 or 100 to 200) change is exponential. The low end requires "organizational triage" as the intervention protocol to reverse the increasing state of entropy. At the high end, change or synergy is evolving exponentially as well. The tipping point is 31 points – below it is easier to degenerate into entropy and above it is more natural for positive development to occur. At this end, the "high performance organization protocol" is an intervention to increase or maintain a synergistic state.

Knowing where the workgroup or organization is on this OUI spectrum is helpful in establishing an intervention plan and determining the MVP reaction time allowed. The further out to either edge of the OUI, the shorter the MVP formation time and communication increases in its importance of disseminating information.

Communication becomes much like the human circulatory system that removes damaged tissue from a bruised area. Contention between two work groups, entropy, is a form of an organizational bruise. The intervention is to increase communication or circulation to the damaged area. The MVP template directly affects the efficiency of this "healing" process. The "purer" the communication, as refined by MVP, the better the intervention and success.

Organizational Architecture: Process

Process, the fourth component of organizational architecture, is probably the best known and most talked about in corporations worldwide. Processes can be informally passed on by word of mouth, and subtly imbedded into the culture or even built into the fabric of the structure. Processes can be very formal and become organizationally institutionalized in themselves such as Right First Time, Quality Assurance,

Theory of Constraints, Six Sigma, and Lean Manufacturing. Predictable implementation success in all cases relies on the sponsorship of the leadership and the change agents who introduce and implement the new processes. It's all about the skill of these people to communicate – prepare and deliver clear, compelling messages to the target of the change. MVP stands tall as a significant contributor.

Organizational Architecture: Intellectual Capital Transformation to Organizational Intelligence

The last dimension of organizational architecture is the dynamic of transforming Intellectual Capital (IC) into usable Organizational Intelligence (OI). Thanks to the research and learning by organization behaviorists, organization developers and orgopathists[1], the mystery of how organizations develop and become greater than the sum of their parts is revealed more and more every day. This dynamic is what gives an organization its ability to compete against the challenging economic and entropic forces. It is how a company can survive and even excel in the jungle of larger competing companies

---

[1] **Orgopathy (ôr' gŏ pə thē) n. [org + pathy]** *The diagnostic, prescriptive, curative, therapeutic, and/or other organizational interventions that would act to restore, preserve and optimize and organization's health and purpose.*

and well-funded start-ups. Theoretically, if you have enough money any business is replicable in terms of equipment, processes and products. What can't be stolen or duplicated is the organizational intelligence that emits from the conversations between two or more individuals (intellectual capital). Restated, intellectual capital resides with the individual but organizational intelligence is generated from the *conversations between* the individuals. The quality of this organizational intelligence is dependent upon communication skill. Communication is the key to organizational intelligence. This underlines once again, the power and value of MVP.

> Organization intelligence is generated from the conversation between two or more individuals (intellectual capital).

4

Motivation

Motivation in the MVP approach is very "up close and personal." It is not about how to motivate someone else. It's all about *you* and *your* motivation toward *others*.

Experts in organizational behavior largely agree that supervisors cannot directly motivate employees to change their behavior. They do recognize the individual has the power to self-motivate. However, the supervisor can set up the work environment to encourage individuals to access greater (or lesser) motivating behaviors. For example, a common motivator is fear of being fired (negative motivation) followed by the desire to maintain a current lifestyle (positive motivation). If a supervisor threatens dismissal if the work group does not meet a deadline, this would trigger each employee's job preservation motivator. The employee's deliberate behaviors adjust to assure job continuance. The point is that the supervisor sets up the environment or work condition that causes the employee to access a desired motivator, which in turn changes a behavior. The employee selects the motivator that acts to address his or her own desired behavior. Therefore, a boss cannot motivate a subordinate as in the 40's and 50's management mindset, which was, "what I say goes." Through "servant leadership," the supervisor creates an empowering work climate that encourages the employee to select an optimum motivator to create excellent work behavior and, as a result, improves performance.

The "M" in MVP is about selecting a desired motivator that will keep *you* on course as you navigate the uncertain rapids of your upcoming dialogue. To be more specific, the person with whom you will be communicating will easily read the motivator you select. It is instinctive. Just as a dog can detect if you are afraid of it, another human can sense what is motivating your conversation with him or her. Picture your child carelessly spilling grape juice on your favorite antique dining room chair. If your subconscious motivation is to punish, your child will recognize the exchange as "pay back." Even though you unemotionally examine your motivation *after* you cool off, and you recognize the motivation should have been to make this a *teaching moment* for your child to learn to be more careful; it's too late. The damage is done. In the moment, the child senses your real motivation and goes into a defensive mode that only acts as a further disconnect. The teachable moment is not accessible under this scenario.

If we act on our emotions – anger, fear, frustration, embarrassment – we are not likely to get the desired outcome, even if we did get attention. Our emotions or feelings are not wrong; it is how they are managed *prior* to the event that is most important. The process of deferring that response until you identify a positive purpose or motivation can put your destructive or dysfunctional emotion in check.

The motivation in MVP can also be expressed as "what is my purpose or motive?" Simply put, what am I trying to accomplish with this conversation? It should reflect something that the other person can understand or easily grasp.

> Motivation in MVP is expressed as, "What is **my** purpose or motive?"

To be motivated to create a "dynamic synergistic state of cooperation," with someone is a very accurate, even noble motivation. However, if it can be reduced to more common language, such as "getting us to work well together," it will be easier to recall when you're under the pressure of the moment and will "bleed through" as being sincere to the other person.

Motivations are infinite. You should make a list of positive motivations before you are required to come up with an MVP in a hurry or under pressure. Developing such a pre-MVP motivation list will both shorten the time to establish your MVP and make it more effective. Examples of motivations could include:

Negative Motivations	**Positive Motivations**
To discipline them	To develop them
To prove them wrong	To discuss the information we have
To show 'em who's boss	To serve them
To punish them	To ignore the past and move on
To set them straight	To learn more about them
To status them	To offer to partner with them
To put fear in them	To take them off the "hot seat"
To challenge their laziness	To recognize what they are doing right
To give them a piece of your mind	To recognize their contribution
To let them have it with both barrels	To apologize
To give them threat/warning	To share the responsibility
To prove that I am tolerant of them	To suggest their real value

The chart shows the possible translation from a negative motivation to a positive motivation. This core skill needs developed if the MVP process is to work. To practice, start your own list!

Think of a time when you had a very distasteful conversation with someone – one of your worst interpersonal experiences. What was your motivation – really? Was it negative, a veiled negative, or a positive motivation? Upon reflection, you may realize your negative motivation had set off a chain reaction of unpleasantness. Let's see how Burt Bullinski's negative motivation could start the "domino effect."

Burt Bullinski was every bit his name. Tough, large and intense, he ran a tight ship. He managed a production plant of 385 unionized workers. He knew the contract, backwards and forwards, and he knew the plant.

J.J. Jones, a crusty and especially focused production supervisor knocked on Burt's door jam – the door had long ago become a casualty of one of Burt's moods.

"Enter!" Burt was still reeling from the phone call he had with his executive vice president of operations. The financial approval for an overhead crane replacement had been put on hold, after eight months of vendor meetings and negotiations. Frustration didn't begin to describe his feelings. His cluttered office had wrinkled papers strewn about, along with about four broken phone receivers. It was amazing he hadn't destroyed his newest one. His face was as red as a tomato with a visible blue vein in his forehead. His clenched teeth could grind nails – at least a 16-penny spike!

"Production line three is down again," reported an exasperated J.J. "The bubble gum, bailing wire and duct tape strategy is no longer working. We need parts and a new filling machine." J.J. rubbed his sweaty forehead.

"By the way," J.J. continues, "I just heard George at the southwest plant say that they got their new crane and now they don't lift half as much as we do," he was breathing heavily through his mouth and his eyes were squinted.

With a curled lip, Burt laid it on. "What do you want from me, a crying towel? They're on a roll down the hall in the room marked, 'men.' Come back when you have a solution and not just problems, needs and wants."

STOP! This is when Burt should have checked his MVP before he spoke again; however, he didn't know about MVP and steamed right on ahead.

Burt knew he had gone too far as soon as the last word was said, but what could he do? The damage was already done. He'd just taken out his rage on his best production supervisor who had been doing the impossible for months. He suddenly felt sick to his stomach.

Not knowing about or simply not using MVP is not a pretty sight. Being on the receiving end of an improperly set MVP isn't pleasant either, as J.J. can attest. His solution? "I'm outta here."

What could a possible positive motivation have been for our troubled friend, Burt?

Let's go back to where J.J. told Burt, "…they don't lift half as much as we do." Now, Burt with his positive MVP in place responds:

"J.J., you have been doing a bang-up job keeping our production lines running. As you know, we are in tight times right now," Burt stood behind his desk, pacing. "I really understand your frustration as I just received word from corporate that our overhead crane replacement request we have been working on getting for so long was put on hold yesterday." Burt motioned to the phone, and then put both hands on his hips.

Burt stopped pacing and began to stroke his chin. "What we *do* have is your experience, creativity and your doggedness to get the job done," Burt's tight lips loosened into what might have been a smile as he stood squarely in front of J.J. "What more do we really need? I'll partner with you on this line three problem and deflect any shots at production from corporate. I'll spend what little we have to get the parts you need. I have that level of authority," Burt noticed J.J. sigh with relief. "By the way, let's put in for a new filler machine – can't hurt. And maybe a case of duct tape thrown in as well. Who knows? Thanks for keeping me informed."

"Burt thanks for listening – I just needed to blow off to someone who cared."

Burt's positive motivation was to re-recruit J.J. back into a thankless job. He knew J.J. was the best and was being worn down, as Burt was, from corporate's decisions. Losing J.J… perish the thought.

As you focus on the motivational part of MVP, it acts as the rudder to keep the conversation on course. Without a rudder, the conversation can quickly degenerate into a tangle of meaningless phrases that can set up further misunderstandings. In some cases, political games and negative coping tactics evolve.

Let's look in on a newly minted salesperson, Barry, and see how he's doing in his first month as a pharmaceutical representative.

Barry recently graduated from Pharmacy U, a 10-week sales program (rather a boot camp for drug reps) he took after he finished his marketing degree in college. It's his first day alone without his trainer in this new job. He carefully combed his brown hair and parted it on one side. He seemed fit and focused. With a dark suit, white shirt, and striped tie with his company's colors, he is picture perfect. He has an appointment today with a ninety-plus physician practice – the biggest non-hospital in his region. He did not feel ready and it would be at least an hour before the head administrator could see him.

"Oh, great," Barry said with a sigh. He sat down in the deceivingly hard seat in the waiting area and rifled through old magazines. A rather elderly gentleman with silvery hair watched with interest, leaning forward on his wooden cane.

"Looking for a good read?" the man asked.

Barry smiled. "Looks like I'll be here for awhile. Why do you ask?"

The man leaned in further; Barry leaned slightly back.

"I just finished an interesting book that I wish I had read thirty-five years ago before I became a salesman," Barry's eyebrows raised as the man took a pause, then pointed a finger at Barry. "You are a salesman, am I right?"

"A-absolutely," Barry stammered, "I majored in marketing in college and this is my first sales position."

"And how do you like it in the real world?"

"So far – well, I'll let you know after today," Barry shifted, trying to keep his poise. "What is your book?"

"Here, take it," the old man pulled a paperback from the pocket of his outer jacket and, with a tremor, handed it to Barry.

Barry narrowed his eyes as he read the title aloud, "Before the Call: The Communication Playbook." He turned back to the man. "Good, you say? Why so?"

The man's grey eyes widened with delight. "Well, the tenet of the book is that you must use MVP to be great at relating to others." When Barry looked at him with confusion, the man continued, "The kind of sales you do and I have done is *relationship* sales. We have to be seen as trustworthy and that we care about the customer and put their needs before our own, in order to sell a product and make our money."

Barry looked back at the book, intrigued by the old man's observation. "Maybe this could help me," he set the book in his lap and stared into his palms. "My hands get sweaty before meeting with a potential customer," he said as he rubbed them together. They shined in the florescent light. Barry took a deep breath and looked up at the ceiling, and then continued, "I even dream about the customer the night before a visit. If they show anything besides excitement at seeing me, it ruins my day. I've got a good product that helps people, why is it so tough?"

The senior salesperson sat back in his chair and scratched his forehead. "By the way, I'm Tim," he offered.

"Nice to meet you. I'm Barry."

"I believe if you follow the book you'll find the sales life to be a lot more fun, rewarding and successful," Tim said, pointing at the book.

"Thanks." Barry lifted the book and began to leaf through its pages. A clock on the wall ticked loudly in the bare waiting area, counting away the seconds. At first, he hurried through the reading, but by the end, he leaned over the book, clinging to every word. When he finished he noticed Tim watching him.

"What was your MVP before you read this?" Tim asked.

Barry took a short pause to reflect. "Well, my motivation was to make a sale, my vision was to have this as my number one customer in the long term, and my paradigm – uh, not sure. Maybe it's that doctors are all about building their practice at any cost – it's all about them."

"Interesting," Tim nodded, "I like your aggressiveness, but let's look at it from the doc's point of view," Tim's eyes glowed with excitement. He missed sales, but that didn't mean had lost his selling skills. "To decide to buy something you have to see value in the product and understand what it can do for you, the purchaser." Barry looked at Tim. "Would this shift your motivation?"

Barry put his fingertips together and rocked back and forth. After a few seconds, he abruptly stopped and exclaimed, "I got it, and it's not to make a sale, but to educate or help the doc understand the product and how it can help his patients!"

"By golly, I think you've got it!" Tim responded with a phony British accent. Before he could add more, the receptionist spoke up.

"Barry, the administrator will see you now."

Barry thanked the receptionist then shook Tim's hand. "Thank you."

"When you get a chance, rethink that vision and paradigm of yours." As Barry cleared his throat, Tim said, "best with your career." Before Barry left the room, he gave Tim a thumbs-up sign. As he disappeared into the open door, he took a glance at the receptionist's note pad. At the top in capital letters was, "M – V – P," followed by notes scribbled all the way down. She gave him a wink and he continued on his way, mentally working out his vision and paradigm.

MVP is a useful tool for just about anyone – from a patient to an eavesdropping receptionist to a high level executive. If you communicate, you can use it. And it all starts with a positive Motivation, Vision, and Paradigm.

MVP is the secret formula for building successful relationships beginning with a positive motivation.

5

Vision

The "V" in MVP is Vision. Vision strategically sits in the middle as it anchors the "Motivation" and "Paradigm" and acts as the linchpin to MVP. It is *your* vision for the outcome of your immediate interaction with another person that is critical to your success. As motivation is the rudder, vision provides the desired destination or end for your communications journey. Without a clear vision, the old joke of, "we're making good time, too bad we're lost," becomes reality and the humor of it disappears.

Too often, many use the word "vision" as a noun denoting a mental picture of the future – something that can be described in a couple of paragraphs, framed, and mounted on the wall (for all to ignore). The more powerful sense of the word is, "to vision," a verb denoting the exercise of imagining or dreaming of what the future "needs to be."

In this context the use of vision no longer means "a mental picture," but refers, rather, to the developing faculty that "visioning" draws upon. The question, "What is your vision?" becomes translated as, "What are you envisioning about your future?"

The ultimate visioning outcome is to shift your hope into belief, imaginary thoughts into reality, and business ideas into workable results. Often, practical people and those scientifically trained have the most difficulty with the vision part of MVP. They are most comfortable with facts – things from which they form their belief systems. Vision seems to equate with dreaming about what is imaginary. The vision used in MVP is not to be confused with being "visionary." Vision is the tool to help determine what behavioral path you should take to achieve your desired outcome.

Envisioning in the MVP model typically has a shorter focal length. A vision will have various focal lengths. For example, as applied to your career it should be years in length. However, when applied to MVP it ends with the completion of the immediate conversation. The short focal length allows you to form a very clear vision with rich detail and deep emotional content. For effective application in MVP, visioning must be positive. Therefore, the emotional content must be positive. Let's probe into this further by example.

The page shook as Clara leafed through a sports magazine, her eyes glazed over each word in an advertisement for athletic gear. She could have been holding a gossip column and she wouldn't have noticed; her mind was too busy racing ahead about her upcoming interview. She shut the magazine with a small huff and looked at the ceiling, trying to collect her thoughts. *It would be the job of my dreams*, she thought. Clara had passed the first two screening rounds of interviews and was now to have a final interview with the administrative partner of the firm, known as "The General." Although no one would dare call her that to her face, her reputation was that she looked and acted every part of "The General." She was a no-nonsense, pristinely dressed and socially proper woman who had blasted through the glass ceiling at the age of twenty-seven.

Clara shifted her focus down to the wall in front of her. The waiting room was large with a classic décor of dark wood and brass. A framed poster of a young woman climbing up the sheer face of a large mountain caught her eye. The caption read, "To reach the top you must vision yourself at the top."

"Neat thought," Clara said to herself. She could relate to the woman in the picture. The analogy was straightforward; this job was her mountain, and the first base camp is the job. In the blink of an eye her vision slipped - she panicked. Suddenly

Clara couldn't see herself with the job. She felt she was barely holding on to the "rock face." Her breathing became shallow and fast. If she didn't compose herself, she would have a true anxiety attack.

Clara took a deep breath and closed her eyes. *I am the woman for this job*, she told herself. She could see "The General" as her mentor and the job as her launch pad. She could feel her career skyrocket. Feeling slightly better, she envisioned herself shaking hands with her new mentor, having just finished an exciting interview and getting the job.

The fog of her vision had cleared, and now she could hear her new employer say, "This was a fun interview for me," the General spoke with sincere clarity, "it reminded me of when I was your age and hired by this firm. I look forward to working together toward our mutual success."

Clara opened her eyes and looked down at her now steady hands. She was ready for the interview.

Reflecting on Clara's visioning experience, it's a good reminder that when we're developing our MVP, conditions are not always ideal. Job pressure, the desire to be successful, the emotions of anger, sadness or frustration, and time constraints all represent real life situations where we can become so overstimulated that visioning efforts become very difficult. Over-stimulation acts to fog our vision. We must exercise significant self-control during these emotional times. While MVP is extremely effective, the preparatory phase does require control, or the reining in of your emotions. Emotions can control behavior. Harnessing our emotions is a crucial element to visioning.

> Overstimulation acts to fog our visioning.

Although there are many methods to control our emotions, one quick method is to strengthen our biofeedback loop temporarily. One method is to focus on a button of your shirt – for example, the third button down. If you keep your eye on the button, without talking or making other movements, you will see it move as your chest expands and contracts from your breathing. Concentrate for 30 to 45 seconds until you feel your shoulders and arms start to relax. At this point, start to think of a positive vision of the outcome of your upcoming conversation or interaction. The focus of your visioning effort is on creating your desired outcome of the future interaction.

Do not confuse an MVP vision with a goal. With the MVP approach, a positive vision is the guide of the exchange. Even if the vision is not explicitly clear but you did have an excellent exchange, the MVP served its purpose. You might like to think of a goal as the marker of a desired result or endpoint.

An MVP sets up the dialog process to be more likely to reach a specific goal. The vision part of the process is to set up a condition where the highest probability of an honest, open exchange of information is possible, which in turn helps you to achieve your goal.

Visioning is like getting into good physical shape. The more you consistently practice or exercise, the more fit you become. The more you consistently exercise and practice visioning, the easier and clearer it becomes.

To better prepare for positive visioning, you can practice by creating short visions. Some examples could include:

- *We enjoyed our conversation and mutually look forward to our next one.*
- *We opened up to each other.*
- *My email triggered a very positive response from my boss – she endorsed my idea!*

- *The team is excited to meet weekly to keep up the positive momentum we achieved this session.*
- *It was a positive and exciting conversation.*
- *The selection committee gave my promotion a unanimous "thumbs up."*
- *The committee accepted my recommendation the first time I tried!*
- *I will be asked to facilitate the off-site retreat of my peers.*
- *There will be thundering applause when I finish my speech.*
- *She saw me as worth her time.*
- *Our disagreement will melt away – almost by magic.*
- *My spouse hears me and we are truly one in our decision.*
- *We reconnected.*
- *My potential client will definitely call me back – what a connection!*
- *We shared our feelings honestly and it felt good.*

Create a few of your own. First, think of a few recent conversations and reflect on your vision for them. If you can't think of any just create a few new and basic visions for conversations you plan to have in the near future. You are just getting a head start practicing for your future MVP efforts.

Negative visions are not helpful in the MVP approach. Negative visioning is the misuse of your imagination. To identify threats and fears is helpful but to obsess and form a negative vision goes beyond usefulness. Some negative visions might be:

- *I hope I don't raise his emotions to a boil.*
- *I'm not going to cry this time.*
- *I never get a word in edgewise – what a motor mouth!*
- *He never gives me the time of day.*
- *I must be nuts trying to talk with her – she never listens.*
- *Well, here goes nothing!*

> Negative visioning is the misuse of your imagination.

For many, it is easier to make a list of negative visions than positives; for people with sensitive phlegmatic temperaments (which are many of us) we don't easily forget the negative experiences that can easily trigger or translate into future negative visions. To overcome this negative conditioning, use the following technique: After you have established your positive vision and before the conversation, simplify the vision into a terse statement. Say this vision piece of your MVP aloud to yourself several times (out of earshot of others, of course) if possible. For example, your vision might be, "I am going to enjoy this conversation." Keep your vision short so you can retain it throughout the conversation. As you repeat this vision phrase to yourself aloud, you will begin to believe yourself when you hear yourself say it. To keep focused, emphasize a different word each time. For example, "*I* am going to enjoy this conversation,"; "I *am* going to enjoy this conversation,"; "I am going to *enjoy* this conversation," and so on. A rule of thumb is that the more negative your experience has been with this situation or type of person in the past, the more times you will have to practice repeating your vision statement. You may often have little or no time to practice your positive vision statement right before the event but you should take every opportunity to practice speaking your vision into reality.

A quick method to determine the number of times to repeat your vision statement is to ask yourself, on a scale of one to 10, how concerned you are about your upcoming conversation. A 10 being, "I'd do almost anything not to have this conversation," a five being, "wish me luck," a three being, "this should work," to a one being, "I really look forward to enjoying this conversation." Take the number that best represents your concern and multiply that by 10 – repeat your vision to yourself that many times. However, a score of "one" does not need to be practiced at all – just have fun and enjoy the conversation.

As previously mentioned, the MVP process gets easier with practice. Therefore, the vision-forming part requires much practice to form a clear picture of the result of your future communication, to do so quickly and execute it well. Some may give up prematurely if they find the MVP effort too difficult to execute. The visioning part of MVP is most often responsible for this frustration. A true loss.

The more you practice, the easier it will become. This is extremely vital when you're under the pressure of a tough topic that with a short period for preparation. In such a situation, practice pays off – it needs to become as close to a knee jerk reaction as possible.

Once you learn to vision, you need to apply your created vision. It does take a bit of boldness at first but as you try it in a real situation – with someone you trust and in a non-pressure situation – you will grow to become more confident.

As you become more comfortable and more successful, try the MVP in tougher and more stressful situations.

Learning MVP is like the process of learning a foreign language. Your first attempts to speak with someone with your newly learned language are often awkward – even embarrassing. However, an interesting dynamic occurs in that the listener never makes fun of or belittles the poorly spoken language. Instead, they encourage the effort and are appreciative of the attempt regardless of the level of proficiency achieved. Using MVP will have similar results. The receiver of the message will be sincerely appreciative of your effort.

Journaling your MVP efforts and outcomes is a technique that can expedite your mastery of MVP. Do not confuse keeping a journal with keeping a diary. This type of journal briefly notes the target of the conversation – a person's name, the situation that generated the need for the conversation, and the communication vehicle used – cell phone, email, text message, letter, etc. Then note your MVP going into the conversation and the outcome of the conversation. Over time, you'll likely reduce the number of entries and just note your exceptionally excellent results and the very awkward exchanges with notes on what to do better next time.

To illustrate the power of visioning practice, try the following. You'll need:

- A pen or pencil.
- Five blank sheets of paper (at least eight inches wide).
- A visioning object (examples might include a coffee stirrer, a plastic knife or fork, an iPod, etc) which is six or less inches in length.

Exercise Instructions:

1. Label each of the sheets of paper with Trial 1, Trial 2, Trial 3, etc.
2. Take the visioning object and study its shape, size and length.
3. Place it out of your direct sight.
4. Mark on the piece of paper marked, "Trial 1," and mark your estimate for the length of the object. For example:

Trial 1

[ ]

5. Overlay your object between your trial lines and mark how close you came to the actual length.
6. Try it again. A visioning technique is to look at the middle and allow your peripheral vision to work. Remove the object and see it in your mind's eye. Look at the object again and look away. If possible, break it into mental parts. When you have a clear vision, mark it on the "Trial 2," sheet. Getting better? Be careful not to use your fingers or a point on the table as a reference. Yes, this is estimating but effective estimating is true visioning.
7. Repeat as Trial 3, 4, 5 etc. until you can replicate the length of your visioning object.

This exercise has a right or wrong outcome – either you were able to mark the length or not. This helps you gain boldness to declare or commit to your vision by marking down your envisioned length. As you repeat the process, you will gain belief in your capability to vision – a core component of positive visioning needed in your MVP. This belief then transforms into visioning strength that increases consistency in your MVP efforts.

Vision in MVP is not as simple as, "you think it, you achieve it." Don't we all wish this could be true? However, to vision is to create a clear mental picture of the outcome that you desire in the future interaction. If you keep this picture clear in your mind throughout the conversation, you will be able to determine, in real time, if you are making progress – and what conversational behaviors are taking you closer to your desired destination or away from it. This use of vision becomes an excellent feedback tool to confirm that your MVP is tracking properly.

In summary, visioning is the art of seeing in your mind's eye the destination of your communication journey.

6
Paradigm

Let's observe a leadership class solve a riddle.

"Two men died in a cabin in the woods. How did they die?" The presenter looked around the room. The class stared blankly at him. "If you have the right *paradigm*, you can solve this puzzle in seconds. If not, you cannot solve the puzzle," some of the participants shifted in their seats. "You may ask any question you'd like, except the obvious one of, 'how did they die?'" The questions started to come in fast and furious.

"Were they sick?" one woman asked.

"No," replied the instructor.

"Did they die in a fire?" asked another participant.

"No, but there was a fire after they died."

Fifteen pairs of eyes darted around the room.

"Did they know each other?"

"Yes, in fact, they worked together."

"Did they die at the same time?"

"Yes."

"Were they poisoned?"

"No."

"Did they die of foul play?"

"If you are asking were they killed by a criminal act, the answer is no."

"Were they lost?"

"No, in fact they were very skilled in navigation.

"Did they have enough food to eat?"

"Yes, they had recently had breakfast together."

"Did a bear or wild animal eat them?"

"No."

"Was weather a factor?"

"Yes it was. It was a nasty day with winds and severe thunderstorms."

There was a short pause. The air was thick with thought.

"Did a log fall on the cabin?"

"Yes, but it was not the cause of death."

After another pause, the presenter spoke up.

"Let's examine the paradigm you are using to help you along," he said. "Describe your cabin to me."

An executive in the rear of the classroom said, "A log structure with a stone fireplace. Maybe a table and a couple of chairs, a front porch with a rocking chair…"

“Ah, excellent,” replied the instructor. “A clear paradigm of a cabin; however, may I suggest this paradigm will not allow you to solve the puzzle? As you know, a paradigm is a lens or mental model through which you view information. Let me help you switch the paradigm, or your lens, in order to make my point. What types of cabins are there?”

“A brick cabin,” said one eager class member.

“A stone cabin?” suggested another.

“A metal cabin…”

From the back of the room came another comment. “We’re talking cabin, not a recreational vehicle, right?”

There was another long pause. The instructor smiled and offered another clue.

“Would it help you if I was to suggest this cabin was unique in that it had a row of windows along two sides?”

“How about a boat cabin?” suggested one of the younger members.

“In a forest?” The ripple of laughter abruptly stopped when a young executive interrupted, “I’ve got it! A plane crashed into the cabin.”

Everyone in the room looked to the presenter, hopeful for the answer.

"Interesting, but no cigar," he told them as they stared down at their desks.

The participant who offered the boat cabin idea spoke up again. "It *was* a plane crash; the two men were pilots," all eyes turned to him. "The cabin was a plane cabin and they crashed into the woods."

"Congratulations, you are correct," praised the instructor. "How did you come to solve it?"

"Well boat cabin didn't work and when I heard the idea that the plane crashed into the cabin, I thought of a plane cabin with two men or pilots crashing into the woods from a severe storm. I might add for those who thought my boat cabin was funny that the answer was 'plain' after all." Groans filled the classroom.

Although a rather straightforward puzzle, it illustrates a clear point that if the person does not have the right paradigm, the person cannot solve the puzzle. With the correct paradigm, it is easy to solve in seconds.

Paradigm is the third component of MVP. Granted, the term "paradigm" is often misunderstood and overused in today's workplace. To extend our analogy with motivation being the rudder and vision being the destination, the paradigm is the compass. It constantly confirms you are heading toward your port of call.

As a brief review, a paradigm is a mental model or a lens that we use to understand what we see or think. The class's mental model of the cabin was a structure that was wooden, rough, etc. The word "woods," triggered the paradigm of a cabin to be a traditional log cabin home.

Paradigm is the lens that you use to view an upcoming event - it can color, distort, clarify or shift your thinking.

We literally use hundreds of paradigms every day. We use them as time savers and short cuts for making decisions. When a new college professor walks in the first day of class, each student forms a paradigm about this professor. By just looking at this instructor, how they carry themselves, dress, their hairstyle, race, sex, and many other almost unidentifiable factors, we very quickly form a paradigm about this person. It can take weeks, if ever, to shift this instantly formed paradigm. As a result, all of this person's comments, assignments, and lectures filter through this paradigm, and our opinions about this individual skew accordingly. Let's see how Sam's first impression of his new boss affects their relationship.

It was his second day on the job and Sam had yet to meet his section's manager, Rupert, who had been in China when Sam was hired. Immel, Sam's supervisor, promised that Sam would really like Rupert, a true servant leader who was caring, yet slow to be emotional. He was a good listener, a technical expert and a patient teacher. On that second day as Sam walked by Rupert's office, he noticed the light on. Grinning with confidence, he looked forward to meeting Rupert and started for the door.

As he approached, he heard a hoarse voice coming from Rupert's office. Immediately recognizing this was not the time to introduce himself, Sam hurried past the door. The yelling had been so loud he couldn't help but hear some of the dialog.

"I'm done with you, your sloppy unprofessional staff and your failure to follow protocols – it's criminal!" Rupert paused as though listening to the other end. He then unleashed another volley of even harder words upon the listener as Sam quickly disappeared around the corner. *Is that the servant leader I've heard about*? Sam had no further time to reflect as he entered a weekly staff meeting.

Immel began. “Rupert is back from China and will be joining us this morning.” There was an excited murmur among the room, loud enough that no one heard Sam mutter under his breath, “Oh, this will be interesting.” Immel continued his meeting protocol.

Shortly thereafter Rupert took a seat next to Sam. Rupert was short and stocky with Popeye-like arms (without the tattoos). He grabbed Sam’s hand and shook it ferociously.

“So you’re Sam, the new kid on the block – welcome aboard!” Rupert gave him a playful smack on the back. “I’ve heard great things about you.” Sam’s whole body shook, but he couldn’t tell if it was the handshake or the fear that he might explode again.

Rupert was every bit an intense but caring man throughout the meeting. Sam could see the team’s positive response to his leadership, but was still waiting for the other shoe to drop and for the real Rupert to show himself.

For the next several months, Sam worked from time to time with Rupert. He never saw “that man” he witnessed on his second day of work, but was still reserved toward his manager. One day, Rupert asked Sam to accompany him on an important customer’s call a couple of hours from the office. The trip took all day, and was so interesting and enjoyable that on the way back, Sam decided he needed to know about that fateful day. He was "fifty-fifty" that Rupert was either a closet bully or a servant leader. He had truly grown to like Rupert and felt their relationship had developed so Sam was relatively comfortable asking him about it.

"Rupert, would you mind if I ask you a rather personal question?"

"Fire away," said Rupert.

"When I first came here, I walked by your office and couldn't help but overhear you ripping someone a new one on the phone," Rupert glanced at Sam from the driver's seat. Sam continued, "You weren't mincing any words…"

Rupert cut him off. "You heard that, did you?" he sighed and stared straight ahead. "I'm still upset about it."

Sam noticed Rupert's knuckles turning white on the steering wheel. This was it. He hit the button.

"My seven-year-old son is fighting cancer and recently had to have surgery. The lead doctor was calling to report that the unusual pain my son was experiencing had been from a surgical sponge, something they had left in by error during the initial surgery," Sam's eyes widened and he immediately felt guilty about his preconceived notions. Rupert continued through a tightened jaw. "They had been in a hurry and didn't follow the protocol as fully as he had initially suggested. He called me that morning to let me know they needed to go in again to retrieve the sponge."

Sam looked at Rupert, unable to reply. He couldn't imagine the amount of stress Rupert must have been going through, and realized he himself might not have handled such a phone call with even half the control Rupert had that day.

Sam's initial paradigm of Rupert was very hard to break. A paradigm is not just an opinion, point of view, an understanding, or philosophy. It drives a person's thinking, or more precisely, an interpretation about an event that in turn creates an emotional response, which yields a corresponding behavior. This process is the Response Cycle – in order to inspire change, you must understand what is driving the behavior. It is easier to understand the model pictorially presented as shown on the next page.

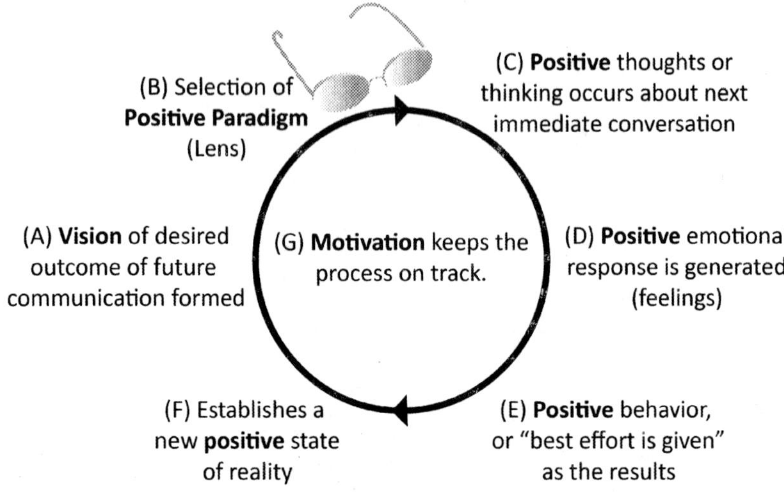

The vision (A) of the positive outcome triggers or sets in motion the search for the most positive and useful paradigm (B) to realize the vision. The selected paradigm becomes the glasses through which we "read" the other person or form our thinking (C) about the upcoming communication encounter. This thinking or interpretation of the vision will create an emotion (D) or multiple emotions depending on your visioning skills. The emotions (of which there are hundreds) generate the actual verbal or written communication behavior (E). Such behavior creates a new relationship state (F) either positive or negative. Following the MVP model, it will consistently be a positive result. Motivation (G) generates the energy and creativity to keep the process on track.

The model demonstrates the strong influence of the paradigm or this “processing lens.” Often, it contributes significantly to the outcome of the communication event – even before it begins. Although yet unproven, users have even suggested it can literally define the probability of a communication outcome’s success.

Let’s examine another scenario. Ms. Brown sat at her small desk covered by neatly arranged lesson plans, handouts, and student files. It was the first day of school, and any minute her new fifth-grade class would be ushered through the door. She flipped through records of her students, trying to make a guess of what the year would bring. The last file was the thickest, with multiple sheets of loose paper covered in scribbled comments from previous teachers. The boy’s name was all over – Johnny. “Johnny is disruptive in class.” “Johnny refuses to hand in homework.” “Johnny threw a spit ball at the wall and left a blue stain – he must have dyed it by eating a blue piece of candy…” Ms. Brown began to leaf through the comments, some of them repeating from year to year. The transcripts indicated he was a C-average student. *At least he has potential*, she thought. (Note: This is the beginning of a positive paradigm of Johnny.)

Let's take a step back. Ms. Brown's MVP is critical not only to make the first day go well (it sets a positive paradigm of Johnny), but because she will ultimately set Johnny's paradigm about her as his teacher. He'll place her somewhere on the spectrum from friend, to someone who seems to believe in him and his potential, to a person he will have to be cautious around or even worse, as an opponent. Where Johnny places Ms. Brown will have a significant impact on the year's learning, and possibly even influence Johnny's life success.

People of all ages can "read" other people's paradigms. It bleeds through even when we desire to keep them out of sight. Would anyone believe that Johnny would miss a paradigm used by Ms. Brown that he was a bad boy who needed to be controlled and would never excel at anything? Or, would Johnny miss Ms. Brown's paradigm that she felt he was worth her time and that they would have a good year? Given the latter paradigm, Ms. Brown would form a positive MVP for her first encounter with Johnny. She would have a vision for a positive friendship and learning partnership to be established and using the positive paradigm would carefully read Johnny's file looking for a logical point of "intervention" to connect with Johnny positively. This thought would yield a feeling from the desired end of the emotional spectrum that in turn would result in a warm, smiling welcome to Johnny from Ms. Brown. Life is good.

To further illustrate the power of the model it can also be used for the remediation of past communication errors or issues.

Having consulted with many organizations, it is normal for our business relationship to start with, “We are having a difficulty with a member of our team.” They go on to pronounce the diagnosis as, “He doesn’t play well with others. It seems to be a personality problem which results in poor communications.” They add the final bit of urgency and request as, “This will be his last chance; can you help us?” Soon into the conversation I will inquire, “How long have you experienced this problem?” In many cases the response is, “For as long as I have known this individual which is many years.”

They have obviously thrown in the towel, given up hope, come to the end of their rope, mentally fired the person or quit trying on their own, regardless what term they use. Yes, years of therapy, skill training, and/or mentoring would probably be helpful. However, they are fresh out of patience, which also means they don’t desire to “invest” any more dollars in this individual. They have largely gotten over any guilt they may have had in allowing this problem to continue so long and have made peace that this person can "go" if nothing else can be done. This limits intervention options to very few.

Operant conditioning is sometimes helpful. Recall Pavlov's Dogs - operant conditioning is the process of changing (aberrant in this case) behavior by rewarding or punishing the subject each time a behavior or action is performed until the subject "gets the message," that the behavior will result in either pleasure or distress. Obviously, this requires time and discipline by the employing agency – of which is neither typically available nor practical.

A second intervention option is to increase the target individual's "dissatisfaction" about their negative behavior. Often due to unique individual characteristics, lack of consistent behavior feedback or cultural misalignment or some combination of these, this individual is in "misery". However, change in behavior only occurs when the individual becomes "dissatisfied" and not when they are in this state of misery. The difference between "misery" and "dissatisfaction" is simply *vision*. When the individual can visualize a better state than the current state, the person becomes dissatisfied and ready to absorb change.

For example, an elderly retired couple lived in the tough part of town and every year added another lock to their doors to keep people from burglarizing their home. They were scared and in misery. Their adult daughter suggested they move to a condominium in her quiet suburban community where no one locks their doors and the residents look out for each other. A vision of a better life. The vision of a safe neighborhood creates dissatisfaction with their current home and they are ready to consider relocating.

A third intervention is shifting the individual's paradigm. With this approach, the individual inserts a new lens for reviewing ongoing behavior. No external person has to give consistent feedback or be directly involved. This individual self-corrects and would behave differently due to a different driver (emotion) established by a different way of thinking about a given situation because they looked at the event through a different, more powerful and useful paradigm. The result – a consistent change in behavior with little outside coaching needed once the paradigm has been shifted using "dissatisfaction" as the catalyst. MVP addresses the communication issue in which all three positive elements (Motivation, Vision, and Paradigm) surface in development.

The only other intervention needed is to convince the "management" and their peers that change has occurred and they should look for the change, recognize it, and reward it. In other words, give it time and look for the positive change – do not prematurely "fire" the individual. If the individual has already been "fired" by the organization, the paradigm shift will only be of value for that person's next job and employer.

The same paradigm model answers the age-old question, "To motivate a person to perform differently, do you address their attitude or behavior?"

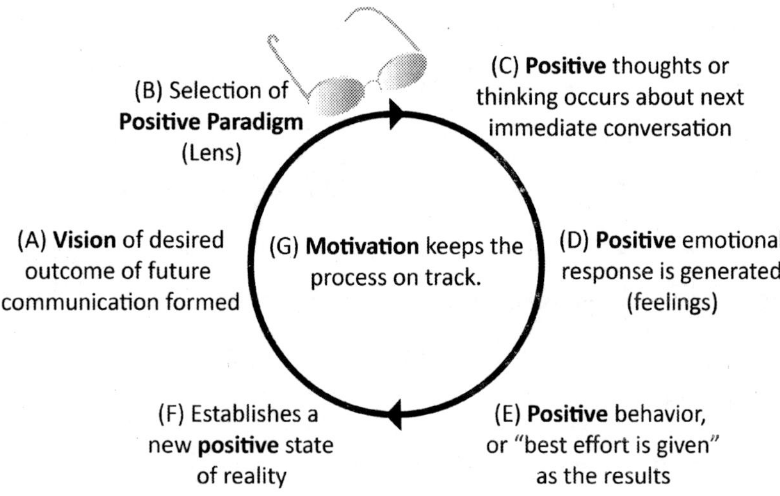

Elements (A) Vision, (B) Paradigm, (C) Thoughts, (D) feelings and (G) Motivation constitute "attitude." Elements (E) Behavior and (F) New State of Reality or Event, are behaviors. As a manager, legally and ethically you can only address a person's behavior. You pay wages for performance or behavior. Your "employment contract" with the employee is for work behavior. Attitude is only of concern when it causes behavior to become substandard. For example, a clerk may be angry and dislike the customer; however, as long as the clerk's behavior is polite, positive and meets customer service standards, the clerk's attitude is off-limits to the supervisor.

Without a question, attitude influences behavior. Using the model, the behavior is in response to feelings or emotions. To discipline is to address and extinguish negative behaviors. To develop is to encourage desired positive behaviors. We must be careful not to confuse attitude and behavior. To smile is a behavior. Happy is an attitude.

Shifting a paradigm is what shifts our thinking, which shifts our feelings and ultimately behavior. Therefore, this becomes the power component of MVP. To shift your paradigm will shift your communication behavior and success.

As a leader, you can venture into the paradigm world and mentor or coach to improve the behavior of others by adjusting their paradigm. A particular paradigm will influence a particular behavior. To find the direct relationship is the key and job of the leader developing the individual. This process is part science and part art. Trial, test, elicit feedback and try again is the only way to get it right.

The paradigm in MVP is like vision. It is very complex and a challenge to dissect the dynamics as it affects people and the work place. However, for MVP it only needs to be addressed at the surface level. As with developing vision, shifting a paradigm takes practice. One method to begin the process of learning to shift a paradigm is on the next page.

Paradigm Shifting

Start Here:

Current State:

No MVP used.
Business as usual.

Paradigm:

Linda is all about Linda;
she is cold and aloof.

Conversation:

"Excuse me, Linda; do you have some time to discuss our project?"

"I'm busy trying to get my part done!" Linda replies, "Stop back when I have time."

Paradigm Analysis:

Linda is busy.
She is driven for results and doesn't want to waste time.
Linda sees her job as #1 - not socializing.

New Revised Paradigm Analysis:

Linda needs dedicated time to do her job so she will want to control her own schedule.
Linda likes closure/results so any request must respect her need for results. Linda wants to see a purpose for her work.

Positive MVP:

M - To tap Linda's expertise.
V - We will connect well.
P - Linda is driven to contribute.
She is dedicated to the company.

New Conversation:

"Linda, I'm working on the budget for our project. I need your input to see if my final numbers match your numbers. I think it will take 15 minutes or so, is this a good time or can we schedule a time?"
"I could use a break," says Linda.
"Let's do it now."

Key: ▲= Paradigm Shift Point

Don't we love it when a plan comes together! Although this is only a contrived example with an excellent result, it does illustrate the process of shifting a paradigm. You need to take the time to flow it out. At first, it will be awkward and best done on paper. As your skill increases, you can do it in your head real time. Ultimately, it is very doable to get your MVP preparation time down to as quick as three seconds. Even for the infrequent tough communication encounters, it can be done in minutes, not hours.

To get started in shifting paradigms, the following provides some examples.

Negative Paradigm	***Positive Paradigm***
She's a snob.	She is shy.
She wastes my time.	She is a valuable resource to be tapped.
He's lazy.	He's never overwhelmed and is available to help me.
He lives in his silo.	He is my partner.
He's a hell raiser.	He takes risks for us.
She holds grudges.	She is our historian.
He's always competing with me.	He sets the right pace for us.
She doesn't respect me or see my value.	I am a servant leader there to support her.
He's incompetent.	He's a work in progress.
He's a lone ranger.	I'm his safety net.
He's a cocked gun with a hair trigger.	I'll provide the right target.
She looks for a fight.	She's developing my conflict management skills.

As the compass for our communications, the paradigm plays a key role in refining our communication skills. If your communications/relationships are not improving and/or your MVP is not working for you, as it should, go first to your paradigm. If it's not your paradigm, work backward through vision to motivation. The simple test is to ask yourself, "Do I like this person?" If your response is a bland or negative one, then ask yourself, "What do I feel about this person going into the conversation/communication?" If it is negative, then most likely your paradigm needs work.

If your MVP is not working, first check your paradigm and work backwards to vision and lastly motivation.

7

MVP De-Railers

So far, MVP appears rather straightforward. If it is as simple as 1-2-3, why doesn't everyone use it? MVP is an essential template taught in such avenues as Leadership Flight School™, Choose to Lead™ seminars, communications workshops and Peer Leadership™ sessions. The breadth and depth of feedback about the MVP technique has been rewarding and even exhilarating. However, as in refining any new skill, it's important to examine the factors that can get in the way of your success or take you "off track". We not so fondly call them MVP "de-railers". They significantly affect both personal and corporate communications.

The easiest and most universal place to begin is with the people themselves. We have found, looking at an extensive database of well over 10,000 cases, that the following factors influence MVP development and its use:

- Temperament
- Personality
- Vector/Valence
- Stress Quotient

- Conflict Management

Temperament

The temperament model most widely recognized is the DISC. It measures the basic need of the individual. Temperament is very stable and is the foundation on which our personality forms. It is not unlike height in that at a certain age we reach our height that takes us through life. Yes, one can bend down or stand on a ladder to reduce or increase altitude but the basic height is established. Personality, ever simplified, is like body weight. It will fluctuate over time and does relate somewhat proportionally to height.

Knowing your temperament and the temperament of others is helpful to connect and apply MVP more easily. A short online inventory can measure your specific temperament. For now, let's take a closer look at DISC. For ease of discussion, "D" stands for the "Driver" temperament; "I" for "Influencer;" "S" for "Stabilizer;" and "C" for "Conscientious." Everyone has some level of each of the four temperaments. It is the extent at which they are dominant, the combinations of these and how they interface with others that sets up the dynamic.

A strong or dominant "D" tends to go to the bottom line without working the process steps to get there. Shortcuts to get the result are important. MVP is about results… and *process*. This does not suggest dominant "D's" can't learn and use MVP. It is only that they need to make peace with themselves that the value of MVP and the benefits obtained exceed the self-control required. Once D's "lock on" to MVP they use it very effectively.

The dominant "I" enjoys the pleasure of speaking many words per day. Although "D's" can shut people down by their intensity, dominant "I's" can wear people down with their excessive verbiage. They can eventually get to the point, but on the way, they'll explore numerous pathways, cart ways, alleys, side roads… you get the picture. They often live for the moment, so they easily forget MVP or get lost in their verbal journey. An "I," does enjoy the MVP approach once learned, as it makes talking with others even more positive.

Dominant "S," temperaments respect process and are excellent "readers" of people. They are the most consistent with the use of the MVP. This is meaningful in that a majority of people have some dominant "S" temperament, approximately 55% of the general population. Anyone can have one or combinations of two or three dominant temperaments; however, the dominant "S" person does not like unplanned change or unleashed, uncivilized emotional responses.

The dominant "C" temperament is into detail, can be judgmental of others and often define themselves by the job they perform. When they make a mistake, they are very hard on themselves. These individuals benefit greatly from using MVP, but learning to trust and go with the MVP process can be a challenge.

With this brief introduction to temperament, you can begin to see how different temperaments and combinations of temperaments may find the MVP process to be awkward at the beginning. For example, a high "D" who is trying to connect with a peer who is a high "I-S" can be seen as pushy, insensitive, and even harsh, which requires a higher MVP skill level from the "I-S" individual. Once it is working well, the high "D" will respect the MVP process and begin his journey with it – but it will take longer to become artful.

Another combination, "C-D," while often good with judgment, can be cautious of others and their motives. Their questions may come across as interrogating and "I" and "S" individuals may see them as somewhat edgy. The return on the MVP development investment is great in these cases; however, the "C-D" often triggers the other individual to fall back to a more parent-to-child response that retards their MVP developmental process, much to their frustration.

A colleague of mine stopped me in the hall not long ago and said, "I hear you are writing a book on MVP, which is still elusive at times for me being a DC." He went on to say he had received an e-mail that upset him so much that in a typical knee-jerk response he sent a missile back only to realize he had pushed "send" before checking his MVP. He ended by saying, "tell the reader to 'MVP it' or plan on expensive damage control!"

Another interesting combination is the "I-C". An individual that has both a high or dominant "I" and "C" will act like a high, dominant "D" with all the MVP ramifications of a high, dominant "D."

Probably one of the most beneficial combinations for the use of MVP is when one spouse is a dominant "D," "I-D," or "D-I," and the other is a dominant "S," "S-C," or "C-S." These temperament combinations often find themselves married to one another. Opposites really do seem to attract, but temperamentally wear down over time and become disassociated. Counseling enhanced with MVP significantly increases the probability of a lasting relationship.

Personality Factors

Personality is another complex area that affects MVP usage. Being reserved or shy makes it uncomfortable for a person to communicate easily. However, this does not suggest the individual can't successfully use MVP. To the contrary, it gives them a motivation and a protocol to use to communicate effectively – a solution to their shyness.

Competitiveness is another area that can act to dampen the effectiveness of MVP. This quality bleeds through and can dominate or overwhelm the motivation component of MVP. Although many organizations desire highly motivated people, if not well managed their competitive nature can neutralize the effectiveness of MVP. This competitive individual will need to practice and turn their competitiveness toward themselves and take the challenge to become a MVP master.

A strong egocentric or a person who is self-centered with little or no regard for the interests, beliefs or attitudes of others will find MVP the toughest to use. The sad part is they would benefit greatly in their relationships if they could harness their MVP. However, this personality often doesn't recognize the need and will not easily become "dissatisfied" with their behavior, as we explained in the prior chapter.

A more subtle but just as difficult quality for MVP use is an individual who is too comfortable with him or herself. This dynamic occurs when the individual sets the threshold of learning extremely high. A normal threshold allows a person to be curious and learn from daily events or experiences. These learning events are catalogued and placed into an internal "database" for future reference. The more one experiences and catalogs, the greater the learning. When the threshold is set too high, it takes an extreme event before it triggers learning. What a typical individual learns in a week, may take a couple of months for a person too comfortable with him or herself. This individual's MVP skill develops at a slow rate, if at all.

Being "fixed in belief" or "very principled" in contrast to being "situational" makes shifting a paradigm more difficult. This mental toughness when coupled with a dominant "C" temperament acts to "inhibit" or in some cases even "freeze up" a person's ability to shift a paradigm needed for MVP. Again, practice usually alleviates this blockage to MVP usage.

Being disorganized or not planful slows the speed of MVP formation, even more so if a person has a very dominant "I" temperament that tends to make him or her "live for the moment." The self-discipline required to learn MVP is compromised with these qualities. Practice can overcome this dynamic. MVP can help with work planning and prioritization as a secondary benefit.

If a person has significant nervous tension or is unusually sensitive to stressors, then he or she may have to elongate the MVP process intentionally. If the meeting is to occur shortly, the individual will need to seek a quiet place that does not trigger his or her urgency and has a calming effect. Those with nervous tension should give themselves as much time as possible to develop MVP. If time permits, they should write down their MVP. The very act of writing will slow them enough to get the traction needed to develop their MVP. This process also works well for those who have a conservative mental processing ability.

Any personality disorder affects MVP formation. However, the traits presented here are personality characteristics that can make MVP difficult or awkward to learn.

Vector/Valence: Natural Influence Mode

Numerous organizational factors beyond temperament and personality affect the MVP process. One fascinating dynamic used by organization behaviorists and team builders is Vector/Valence. Although this dynamic is constantly being adjusted within each individual at any given time, every individual will have a specific vector/valence. A positive vector/valence is someone who approaches his or her world from a relationship perspective. The negative vector/valence is someone who approaches their world from the perspective of tasks and output. A negative vector/valence has nothing to do with the term, "negative personality," or "being negative." In reality, an individual with a negative vector/valence can be charming, helpful, etc.

The vector/valence score indicates a person's natural mode of influence and intensity. Think of a magnet. A magnet has both positive and negative poles. It is not a judgment of good or bad ends of the magnet. People are similar in that they have a negative or positive polarity and intensity. Vector/valence is similar to the strength of a magnet. A person's score indicates the intensity of polarity and the influence he or she brings to a "pure" situation. However, in reality, no situation is truly "pure"; prior relationship history, roles we play, informal power alliances, and level of expertise can all "muddy up" the interpersonal dynamics. A person's vector/valence score contributes considerably to the interpersonal dynamics when he or she interacts with others.

As this vector/valence score increases so does the individual's influence on the group dynamic.

Just like a magnet, opposite poles attract. The stronger the magnet or vector/valence, the greater this dynamic. The lowest vector/valence number is ±0.000. This would be like being a piece of steel plate. Both magnetic poles could connect with the steel plate. It is the same in a team setting – all players can easily connect with this low vector/valence person, regardless of their own vector/valence. The individual acts as a bridge or connector between players. For an optimal "natural team", the sum of the members' vector/valences should be as close to zero as possible. We have all felt room vector when someone keeps pulling the meeting their way. Even if you have a low vector/valence, there are numerous techniques to leverage it. For example, two easy vector/valence-enhancing strategies are:

1. Choosing to sit in the room's Power Seat.
2. Taking up physical space by placing your arm over the empty chair next to you.

More vector/valence strategies could easily take up another book.

The application of the vector/valence to the MVP model is this – the lower the sum of the vector/valences of the individuals relating to or communicating with one another, the easier the MVP experience. For example, if five individuals are in a meeting, the closer the sum of their vectors is to zero (0), the more effective MVP will be when used.

For an optimal "natural team", the sum of the members' vector/valence should be as close to zero (0) as possible.

Stress Quotient

A person's Stress Quotient (SQ) also affects the need for MVP in his or her relationship diet. A stress quotient contains three parts:

1. Nervous tension or energy.
2. Self esteem.
3. Sensitivity to emotional stimuli.

The lower the score, the greater a person's sensitivity to stressors. The higher the score (up to a maximum of 27), the more stressors an individual can withstand before he or she feels stressed. As the SQ moves down away from a score of 15, the individual will find that using MVP is a very pleasant and rewarding experience. It provides solace in knowing that the improved communications increased control or influence over relationships. The higher a person's SQ score over 15, the less likely the individual will see the need for MVP, an error of analysis in the least of cases.

Conflict Management

Your approach to managing conflict also influences the development of your MVP. One model of conflict management looks at four modes of response:

- Aggressive/Confrontive
- Assertive/Persuasive
- Observant/Introspective
- Avoiding/Reactive.

As the conflict continues in length and/or intensity, the response will shift. Some individuals start out persuasive and when challenged revert to withdrawal. Others begin with introspection, briefly become persuasive and then ramp all the way up to aggressiveness. There are countless combinations and shift options. On a spectrum of intervention from aggressiveness to withdrawal, the individuals that typically operate in the persuasive, introspective, withdrawal end of the spectrum seem to connect most easily with the MVP approach.

Environment can also make a difference when using MVP. In a relaxed location away from the workplace, it may seem easy to quickly and effectively grasp and use MVP. Back in the workplace, it may seem to become so much more difficult that some give it up. It is like a person that has been cured of tuberculosis only to become re-infected when returned to the same tuberculin environment.

Very few organizational factors exist that are seriously caustic to your use of MVP. However, one difficult factor is when the senior management is mean or bullies their subordinates. Often these isolated individuals have fought their way up to senior management positions. They never become leaders in that they can't amass any followership unless they command it, which just lasts until they leave the room and the employees revert to being just managed. To some degree, MVP does work on these "bully" managers, which makes exchanges less damaging to the individual using MVP. However, the "bully" executive, when taught MVP, uses it as just another put down in his or her arsenal of cruel tools. Reportedly, one subordinate struggling to stand up and make a counter point to his "bully" boss was told, "Before you go any further down this wrong road with me, you'd better check your MVP or you'll be MIA." Workplace cruelty is not just the domain of the "mean" executive, but does influence MVP.

MVP is not capitulation and does not harm your self-esteem. Instead, MVP levels the playing field from a servant leader perspective. It sets up the playing field to be helpful and connected, and enhances the delivery and understanding of a topic.

Work cultures, structures, silos (boundary intensity) and poor processes can also impede the development and use of MVP in a significant way. Its success rests with your skill in applying it to the communication event. Attaining confidence in its application means practice, practice, practice!

MVP is not capitulation and does not harm your self-esteem.

8

Getting Ready

You now know what MVP is, what it does, how it can be de-railed and its place in your organization. This chapter is devoted to preparing you to exercise your MVP.

After you're "ready," the next two chapters will make sure you're "set" and then totally equipped to "go" using MVP!

Getting ready to use MVP is not necessarily time consuming. We don't often want to start to learn a new technique or tool if we don't feel we have enough time to do it right or complete the training. Research shows over 55% of people have a dominant "S" or "C" temperament, according to the DISC instrument. These people are time concerned and may not begin the effort until they feel they have adequate time to complete the process.

To get around this time concern blockage, simply select a time you will be e-mailing someone, calling someone, or having a face-to-face with someone and set your watch for only three minutes. Use one minute for Motivation, one minute Vision and one for Paradigm. Focus on developing your MVP for the upcoming event. Stop in three minutes, even if you are not fully convinced your MVP is as robust or as helpful as you think possible. You might surprise yourself! If you can think of your MVP in less than three minutes then use the additional time and write it down. You can review it later to see if it added value to your conversation and use it as a future reference for an MVP that worked for you in the past.

Getting started is as simple as deciding to use MVP as a tool to enrich your relationships through your excellent communications. Any way you improve your communication leverages your personality, talents and life experiences for better relationships and results.

Any way you improve your communication leverages your personality, talents and life experiences for better relationships and results.

Mastering MVP is not like learning to play the piano, which takes years of practice to become skillful. Literally, the second time you use MVP you will start to experience a remarkable improvement in your communication effectiveness. Give yourself a reward when you use MVP by keeping score - a plus (+) if it seemed better, zero (0) for no difference and a minus (-) if it caused some breakdown in the communication.

A sample score sheet is shown below. Periodically review your score sheet. Is it improving? Does the form of communications make a difference?

Name:	Form of Communication - Category				Score
	Email	Phone	In Person	Other	(+ / 0 / -)
Fred	x				0
John		x			+
Sally	x				+
Bob		x			+
Karen			x		+

One comment I hear rather frequently is that it takes longer to write an e-mail with a solid MVP. However, because the quality has increased, the number of necessary e-mails to an individual slowly reduce, which in turn improves your efficiency.

Set a goal. For example, at 50 pluses (+) calibrate your success. Another goal would be to reset your list at every 25 and calculate the percentages that were pluses. Try to increase your percentage score by category as another goal to achieve.

If you are having a dry spell of several zeros or minuses, take the time to analyze the reason why. Journaling all of your communication events might help your diagnosis.

I've found that the most common reason for MVP failure was that the individual's emotions about the topic overrode their MVP. "I was so p***ed that I didn't give a s*** how I communicated!" Emotions will get in the way of developing and unleashing your MVP. Use the development of your MVP to harness your emotions deliberately, even when you would rather "let 'er rip."

When you take the easy way out and let your emotions dictate your communication style, you will condition the listener to expect poor results. They shore themselves up for another volley of spew and when you do use your MVP, they miss it. It is similar to plugging your ears if you anticipate a large explosion. This most often occurs between spouses and business partners.

Ridicule or embarrassment keeps some people from starting to use MVP. As one person put it, "It was like I was admitting I had a problem talking to others. I never mentioned it again, although I've used MVP for several years."

Another MVP non-starter is fear of failure. Not understanding MVP usually creates this fear. I have never known a positive MVP, in and of itself to cause a breakdown in communications. However, a negative motivation, vision and/or paradigm will not help in any situation.

Not recognizing the need to improve communications can stunt your MVP development. Egocentric people, those too full of importance or obsessed with success, or those who influence through intimidation, often see no need to try MVP. The best recommendation I've heard was, "Try it, you'll like MVP."

Once you overcome any initial fears or blockages, you're ready to ask, "How do I prepare myself to use my MVP?"

To get started, follow these seven steps:

Step 1: Make the decision to use MVP.

Step 2: Check your DISC score. A very dominant "I-S" will connect easily. However, sometimes this temperament connects so well that it feels like he or she already "naturally" uses MVP, when this is not the case. But a dominant "I-S" will enjoy the process.

A dominant "D" will try to cut corners and power through the MVP process. A person of this temperament needs to be more deliberate and write down the MVP before use.

A dominant “C-D” or “D-C” will benefit significantly from MVP especially if this person is in the “up” or “superior” position in the conversation.

A strong or dominant “S” or “S-C” will feel awkward at the beginning but will come online and stay online. This temperament can become the “poster child” of MVP.

Step 3: Select someone to try out your MVP. Don’t initially tell them that they are your trial subject. Select someone that is a dominant “S” or “I-S” or “S-I,” if possible. You want your first experience to show promise and encourage you to try again. A friend is always a safe choice. However, a work associate is even better in that you will not be as tempted to go too deep into the emotional arena, at least not as quickly. A subordinate is also a good pick.

Step 4: Select a friendly topic for your first experience. It should be emotionally quiet, if possible, and free from “drama.” It should not trigger history or past negative feelings. It should not result in a debate or contest of any sort.

Step 5: Select the time for applying the MVP. When you’re under pressure, you won’t do your best. Give yourself an open-ended period for applying your MVP the first few times.

Step 6: Select the location. Excess noise, confusion or interruptions dampen the effectiveness of your early MVP efforts. Part of the learning process is to pick up verbal and nonverbal cues. Verbal cues need relative quiet and a place that does not challenge your concentration. This obviously applies to one-on-one or telephonic communications, which often works well for your first MVP efforts.

Step 7: Write down your MVP. It will take some time to get it the way you want but this effort will place it clearly in your memory, ready for instant recall. Like any new behavior, it takes several times for it to become habitual, which is the end goal.

Now that you are ready and prepared to start, you need to practice. The next chapter will give several examples of practice scenarios. Now practice, practice, practice!

9

Get Set...

You could replace, "get set," with, "practice, practice, practice!" It is only through practice that you'll get set to "go" and utilize MVP masterfully. This chapter contains a series of scenarios that you can refer to and practice as you start using MVP. The best way to read this is to first stand in the shoes of the MVP user and then go back to see it from the non-user's perspective.

You will find a brief background for each scenario interlaced with technical profile information. The MVP will be highlighted before the scenario unfolds, followed by a summary of MVP's impact. The scenarios presented here were inspired from real situations. Obviously, the names have been changed and MVP has been introduced. The profile information, although technically correct, has been appropriately masked.

A careful read and study of the profile information will allow the reader to learn and better understand the dynamics of preparing for a successful connection and communication. The examples contain very typical profiles.

Scenario #1: Subordinate to Boss

Brad sat down in his small office for the first time in three weeks. He worked for an engineering company of 275 employees, with eight branches and a corporate office. The job sure kept him busy. He loved his unpredictable schedule and enjoyed working with his team. He now understood them even better having been to Leadership Flight School™, and they seemed to be responding well to his improving leadership as Program Manager.

As he pulled off his jacket, he noticed there was a slight chill in the air. Out of his pocket he pulled two juice-stained, crayon-drawn pictures – an unsteady, "I love you daddy," from his 5-year-old son and a fresh set of scribbles (said to be a family portrait) from his 3-year-old daughter. He looked to the bulletin board next to his desk. Dozens of similar pictures from his children already covered the board. Brad rummaged through a drawer of office supplies and pulled out two more pushpins, and he pinned the new pictures to the bottom of the cluttered board where they fluttered as the ventilation system roared to life.

When he sat back down, he browsed through the sticky notes clinging to his computer monitor. One in particular, written in red ink, grabbed his attention: "*8:30am. Brief me on*

Limekey project. My office. Pam." Brad narrowed his eyebrows. Pam transferred to this location from the corporate office while he was on his trip. "Huh. Definitely short, sweet and to the point," he muttered. He looked at the clock on the wall. Five minutes after eight. In trying to keep with this Leadership Flight School™ training, he summoned his "MVP man," as he called it. Running his hand through his short hair, he thought about the project first.

The Limekey project is on schedule, he thought, *no problems to date except a delay of a few deliveries of needed machine parts but nothing critical.* Brad leaned forward, resting his chin on his fist. He felt uneasy, sort of a free-floating anxiety but he couldn't put his finger on why…

Let's take a moment to review the profiles of Pam and Brad.

Pam's Profile:

- 35-year-old, single woman. Takes great pride in precision and expects others to as well.
- D-C-s-i; all drive and detail, does not often connect with others.
- Mental agility: 94th Percentile; very fast.

- Vector/Valence: -26.294; very task/results driven.
- Stress Quotient: 8; slightly sensitive and an early reactor to stressors.
- Conflict Management: -10; tries to avoid conflict.
- Strategic, influential, and dedicated to her work.
- Respected by the corporate office as their "can do" manager.
- Views team building as a means to an end, which is results and profit.
- Executes her tasks to the letter.
- Ambition: to become COO of the company by age 40.

Brad's Profile:

- 31-year-old man, married with two children.
- I-S-c-d; relates easily to others. Appreciates process and extreme time constraints.
- Mental Agility: 95th percentile.
- Vector/Valence: +4.617; relationship-based with ability to influence others.
- Stress Quotient: 16; handles stress well.

- Conflict Management: 27; able to confront conflict assertively.
- Verbally expressive but also listens well.
- Parents and in-laws are located near Corporate. Would like to work there someday.
- Attended Leadership Flight School™, where he learned MVP.

Let's hop back into Brad's head while he works out his MVP.

Brad leaned back and stretched his arms upward. Pam's profile is definitely different from his. He had done his homework, learned about Pam's profile, but now he needed to develop his MVP as he had learned in Leadership Flight School™.

His motivation was, well, to not get on her bad side, and set up the future so he could survive… *No, that's a negative motivation.* He'd better try this again.

Maybe she wanted to talk about his team of six – nothing much to talk about – hard working, dedicated. Oh, yeah, there was that bar incident last month with Vince but it was no big deal and he was off the clock anyway. He leaned his forehead into his hand and propped his elbow on the desk. *This has to be a positive motivation*, he reminded himself once again. He found that his "MVP man" kept him honest with his MVP being positive and practical. It had been overwhelming at times but it seemed to resurface to live another day.

His motivation would be to meet and connect with Pam to set up a true partnership. *Yeah, that's it!* His vision was to be partners for their foreseeable future – at least until one of them relocated. A vision in which they would have each other's back and obtain a team reputation of getting the job done – together. *She obtained good experience at Corporate – we can use all the expertise and experience we can get*, he thought.

The big hand on the clock was moving on. "MVP man" was not yet satisfied – where was the "P"? That one was easy – Pam is my boss, so just use the Golden Rule – those who make more gold get to rule. I'll follow her rule. It wasn't a great paradigm but he rationalized that he really didn't know that much about Pam to come up with a better paradigm.

"MVP man" wouldn't let it go. *Ok, let's go over this once more. Pam seems competent, on the way up in the corporate world – she must be doing something right. I got it! She could be my new mentor – why not let her guide my career along?*

When he looked up again it was eight twenty-five. *Well, here goes.* Pam's office was just down the hall. He could see light coming from the room as he stepped out of his own office.

Brad's MVP:

M Connect with Pam and set up a true partnership.

V Their partnership would have the reputation of getting the job done together.

P Pam is Brad's new mentor, who will guide his career.

He knocked on Pam's half-open door. No answer. He peered in; she was absorbed in her laptop. He knocked again and stuck his head in the room. "Should I come back?"

She waved him to a chair without looking up. "I'll be with you in a minute." She didn't raise her head until she was finished typing. "Thanks for coming; it's been a long day already. How long have you been at this location?"

"About three years. Why do you ask?"

"How long did it take for you to get used to it?"

Brad paused, trying to ignore the fact that she had not answered his question. "Several months, I guess."

"I've been here four weeks and," she shook her head. "Never mind. I asked you here to brief me on the Limekey project. Are we on target?"

He nodded slowly, trying to read her body language and tone. *She would've made a great poker player*. "We have some machine parts on back order, but they should be delivered later this week. We'll catch up with no problem."

She stared hard at him as if she was trying to see into his head while tapping her pencil on the desk. She seemed agitated. He took this pause to activate his MVP. "Pam, I'd like to welcome you to our site. It's not large like Corporate but we have a good group of people here – dedicated and hard working. When you have a moment, I'd like to introduce you around to my team. We've all been on the road the last three weeks but everyone will be back by tomorrow. Would you have some time?"

She stared steadily at Brad, studying his face. She paused.

"I think that would be helpful. Yes, when does it work for you?"

"Well, we typically arrive around 7:30. I'll have the coffee ready."

"Seven-thirty would be fine."

"I'll have the group, all six, make a brief status report on what they are doing to get you up to speed – they love to brag and I love to hear it. As time goes on I think you and I will be able to mutually enjoy their success."

Pam stopped drumming her pencil and pushed up her glasses on the top of her head.

"Brad," she cautiously started, "you do know that I took the head of this site over you… don't you? It was slotted for you but I needed a move and this gives me field exposure and experience…" she trailed off.

"I guess I was a bit surprised to hear that someone with your credentials was coming here, but it's all good – I have time, and have several areas of development maybe you could mentor me on – it'll make me better prepared for the next upward move when Corporate feels I'm ready." Brad was feeling his "MVP Man" happily working in overdrive.

"Oh, I see, you see this as sort of a partnership thing," Pam suggested with less intensity.

Noticing her softened tone, Brad went on, "If we have each other's backs we can make this branch even more successful, do we dare dream make this the newest and best performing site – can't hurt either of our careers."

"I like the way you think. It's been cold and windy the last three weeks… I felt I was flying solo."

"Sorry I can't rid this place of the cold and nasty wind, but I'm sure my team and, without question, I would enjoy flying in formation with your plan. Maybe tomorrow you could start to fill us in?"

"Will do," she continued, "Thank you for your hospitality – I feel this may just work." She stood up and shook his hand firmly. A smile had crept up on her face. "See you at 7:30; I've got to get on a corporate conference call. Thanks again." She sat back down and immediately picked up the phone. Though abrupt, Brad felt the meeting went well.

Back in his own office a few hours later, Brad received a copy of an e-mail sent by Pam to her boss at Corporate. It read:

"*I owe you one, you were right. Brad is quite the leader. He asked if I could mentor him – I have much to learn from him – Thanks for giving me this opportunity. Pam.*"

MVP impact subtle? Yes. What would have happened if the MVP was negative, or worse yet, not used at all?

Looking at the profiles of these two people, it would not have been unusual for a contest to take place. Imagine this scenario from Pam's perspective. Pam is sensitive to potential conflict and often uses a preemptive strike to get the upper hand or put her competitor back on their heels. Her DCsi temperament gives her a cautious nature when dealing with others, and at times will even be suspicious. The extreme in this would be paranoia. Care has to be taken not to trigger this tendency because once it is evoked it's difficult to reset a neutral state of believing or trusting in the other person.

Knowing the profile of the person you are relating to allows you to avoid potential land mines in establishing and developing relationships. Brad's MVP allowed him to project a calm, cooperative message to Pam. Obviously, she had a secondary agenda for the meeting that transcended the stated objective, "to review the Limekey project." It allowed her to adjust her paradigm of Brad, which will go a long way toward making their relationship productive long term.

<u>Scenario #2: Peer to Peer</u>

Doug transferred into shipping from the packaging department. In his 22 years with the company, Doug worked in almost every department and done well with each. Today, Doug's supervisor asked him to go over to the motor pool and select a forklift and get started loading the 18-wheelers;

production backed up and the truckers have a schedule to keep. As he stepped out onto the loading dock, he thought about what it must be like to be the supervisor of a department such as packaging or shipping. Staring out across the tall stacks of packaged products, he thought of his daughter and immediately threw the supervisor thought from his mind. Since the accident that left her physically challenged, he can't commit to the extra hours required by a promotion. He and his wife hardly see each other as it is, keeping opposite schedules so their daughter has constant care. Management had approached him a few times to offer supervisory roles, but once word got out that he had no interest, the offers stopped coming. *Just 12 more years 'til retirement*, he thought.

From across the dock, Doug saw a forklift driven by Doc charging toward a trailer. Doc had been in shipping as long as anyone could remember – over 30 years for sure. If it had wheels, he drove it. He kept a good safety record but poor record with his immediate supervisor and the young "whiners," as he called them. They are the ones who don't listen to his stories, ride motorcycles or shoot pool on Friday nights. He works his eight and leaves – he "won't give management another minute of my valuable time."

Doc's mood swings used to intimidate Doug. It wasn't his appearance; when they met he wore the same jeans, large belt buckle and sleeveless t-shirt. The shirt was now a full size too small; it accentuated Doc's large, round stomach. He'd been known to say, "Why work for six-pack abs when I can have a full keg, no effort?" And Doug was used to Doc's long, unkempt hair and well earned broken teeth from a few too many bar altercations. No, he was intimidated the day Doc invited him out for a beer, but in thinking of his daughter, Doug politely refused.

"I don't see you working any overtime, what's one beer?" Doc pressed.

"I just have some things to take care of at home."

"Well, great. That's just great. Go on home and take care of your *things*." Doc stormed off immediately after dramatically punching his time card. Doug wondered what had just happened. Through working with him indirectly off and on throughout his career, Doug learned it was just a part of Doc, and especially after learning about his own personal profile, Doug learned better ways to connect with him.

Doug's Profile:

- 53-year-old married man with one daughter.

- C-s-d-i; detailed, careful, and "close to the vest."
- Mental agility: 84th percentile; above average.
- Vector/valence: -0.072. Can connect with most everyone.
- Stress Quotient: 16; tough minded and able to cope with stress.
- Conflict Management: 68; over twice what is considered adequate.
- Keeps a neat appearance and enjoys working out.
- Internally driven, managed, developed and rewarded.
- Dropped out of college to support his younger brothers and sisters after his father left the family.

Doc's Profile:

- 48-year-old bachelor; divorced 3 times. Ready for his 4th marriage.
- D-I-C-s: can be talkative and energetic one moment then quickly shift to quiet and sullen the next.
- Mental agility: 42nd percentile.

- Vector/valence: -6.024; strongly results-oriented.
- Stress Quotient: 5 (on a scale of 3 to 27).
- Conflict Management: 36.
- Slight hearing loss – speaks louder than most, which occasionally seems hostile.
- Easily crosses the line between persuasive and aggressive.
- Expects others to be interested in his interests and enjoy his "salty" stories.

Doug's MVP:

M To be introduced to his new job assignment.

V To establish a functional relationship with Doc.

P Doc is a decent guy who has real expertise in the motor pool - he can make his orientation to his new job easy.

Doug stepped in front of the charging forklift, trying to get Doc's attention. Not much time for developing an MVP, but Doug's been practicing for several months and thought quickly.

"Whoa, Doug, get outta my way! You could get killed walking out on this runway without a white brain pot," Doc said, referring to the color of hardhat worn by senior management.

“Doc, I know your reputation too well as an ace driver to worry about you not being able to stop,” Doug replied. “But do you have a sec? I have a new assignment and need your advice.”

Doc’s eyebrow raised and his rowdy smile fades as he looks around himself. “You talking to me? I’m no white hat.”

“Yes, you,” Doug responded.

“Well shoot, I’ve got things to lift and move.” Doc reached forward to put the machine back in gear.

Doug got to the point. “I was told to pick up a forklift and start to load the 18-wheelers in the North dock. Can you point me to one of the forks no one else is using?”

Doc left his forklift in neutral, smiled and high-fived Doug. “Well, I’ll be. They sent me some help at last; the cavalry did come just in time – welcome!”

“Just point me to my horse and I’ll be on my way,” Doug quipped.

“Take 36, it has a full tank and just got back from overhaul.” As he got back to his task, Doc loudly muttered under his breath, “They finally sent us real experienced help – not one of those green horns.”

Doug gave a slight, corner-of-the-mouth smile and saluted smartly before going on to find number 36. It went well, he reflected. MVP got the job done. He had never put an MVP together so fast, but his practice paid off.

It's valuable to have some stock, off the shelf, of simple MVPs to use when in a hurry. For example, a quick M or Motivation could be, "to serve," or "assist." A quick V or Vision could be to "enjoy the dialog or communication," or "to set up an excellent connection that is valued by the participants." The P or Paradigm could simply be that this person is "worth my time," or "is valuable to me."

To magnify the power of MVP the next scenario is presented twice – once without MVP and once with an MVP. In addition, this scenario is offered to illustrate its value in preparing to apply even the most simplest of templates – the "broken record."

A template is simply a recipe or process to resolve an issue between individuals. While there are literally hundreds of templates, one of the most basic is the "broken record" template. Use this template only when you are sure of your decision. Seldom does this occur where there is no negotiation room but on occasion, it will happen. It relieves the user of pressure to negotiate or to continually offer counter points that tend to elevate tempers and yield poor results.

Scenario #3: Father and Teenage Son

The father had just purchased a very "hot" sports car for himself, a roadster convertible – red. It was something he desired for some time and, through careful saving with his wife, was finally able to purchase. He promised his wife that Friday night they would have a date and try out the car when they went to the high school football game together.

Unknown to Dad, Hank, his 17-year-old son, invited a girlfriend to the football game. It took a lot of nerve but he finally asked and she said yes. He indicated he had a surprise for their date and it came with four wheels. He couldn't wait to see her expression.

Dad and Hank both work hard for their money. Dad is a young baby boomer, cares deeply for his family, and has learned to defer gratification in order to give the kids what they need and in some cases, just want. Dad is a high "S" and Hank is a low "I" and high "C" on the DISC (further profiling discussion has limited merit for this scenario).

The conversation without MVP and off the cuff responses without a template goes something like this…

It was silent at the table except for the clinking of metal forks to ceramic plates. Mom and Dad sat across from each other and Hank occupied the middle. Hank's eyes shifted back and forth while chewing, gathering his thoughts before he casually brought up his intentions for the evening.

"By the way, Dad, I'm going with Becky to the football game tonight – you know, last year's Homecoming queen?"

"Good for you, Hank! Your mother and I are also going to the game tonight in the new car. We'll see you there."

Hank lowered his eyes. "Well that's what I want to talk to you about… umm… well…" he began to tap his fork on his plate.

"That's a deep subject," his father teased.

Hank blurted out, "I need the car, you see I told her I'd be driving a surprise and…"

"Not so fast, Hank," his father cut him off. "Your mother and I have already planned to use the new car tonight. Sorry."

"Dad, I really need the car – it's my only chance to impress Becky – I promised her." Hank's fist gripped the fork tightly, pointing it to the ceiling.

Dad remained stern. "Well son, why don't you take it tomorrow afternoon and go for a long ride, she'd probably like that."

"No way, I've just got to have the car tonight, it's not fair – you're already married."

Dad dropped his fork, which made Mom jump slightly. She hoped neither of her "boys" noticed. "What's this 'fair' stuff? Your mom and I saved to get this car for many years. When you earn the money you can buy your own car but until that time, beggars can't be choosers."

"I do have some saved up but it would take more like forever to get a car like yours."

"It did take us a long time to earn it as it was, someday you can earn your own sports car."

"Dad, I need it tonight! Why can't you and mom drive the van and take the car out some other time? It will still be there after tonight." Hank's face contorted, his mouth hung open. Several years ago, he would have had tears streaming down his cheeks by now.

"Son, if you keep up this nonsense you'll have no car to use tonight – how about that?" Dad stared straight into Hank's teenaged eyes.

Hank abruptly stood, pushing his chair back hard. "You old fart; you always treat me like crap – why do I even try to talk to you?"

...and the conversation went downhill from there. Now let's see this conversation with an MVP and the "broken record" template.

The 4-step "broken record" template is simple:

1. Prepare your MVP – it must be positive.
2. Clearly make your decision from which there is no negotiation or changing your mind.
3. Listen to the request.
4. Repeat back what the other person requested, using your MVP, and then present your decision at the end.

Repeat steps 3 and 4 until the requesting person gives up, stops challenging the decision or agrees. You need to be cautious that they must be clear there is no other acceptable option you would consider. Otherwise, this is not the correct template to use. You also must stick to the template precisely; otherwise, it could confuse the other person with a mixed message.

Now let's pair it with Dad's MVP and see where the conversation with Hank goes this time.

Dad's MVP:

M Minimize contention in this contentious situation.

V Hank will move on to another option and not dwell on it. Their relationship will not break down over this request.

P Hank is mature enough to work through this situation and is ready for the responsibility of driving a new sports car.

The family of three ate their ground cube steak, homemade fries and mixed vegetables – a Friday night usual. Tim swallowed a mouthful and tried to muster up his courage.

"Dad, would you pass the ketchup?"

"Sure, Hank."

"Thanks. By the way, I asked Becky to go with me to the football game tonight. I was wondering if I could take the new sports car."

"I'm sorry to disappoint you but I already asked your mom to go out on a date this evening to the football game using the new car," Dad said. "As you know, we saved a long time to get this car and I'm sure you'd agree it makes sense for us to be the first ones to break it in. You'll have your chance to use it tomorrow."

Note: So far, the template is not in play as there is no push back or contention.

Hank tried again. "Dad, you don't understand. I promised Becky a surprise with four wheels to pick her up. She's looking forward to it as much as I am."

"Sorry, Hank, our plans are firm for tonight. Why don't you bring her over to see it in the parking lot at the game and set up a time for the two of you to go for a drive tomorrow?"

Note: Still the template is not in play – don't use it until absolutely necessary.

Pulling from his arsenal of excuses, Hank tried to load up on the guilt over his parents. "Don't you realize who Becky is? She's last year's Homecoming queen. The most popular guy in school also asked her to the game but I upped the offer with the promise of an awesome carriage to pick her up. I can't let her down now!"

Note: Hank is ramping up and not budging. Further discussion will turn into an argument – the negative of Dad's MVP. Now it's time to enact the template.

Mom slowed her chewing, watching the conversation carefully. Dad stayed firm. "Hank, I do know who Becky is and I'm excited for your date with her. I also feel your concern that you are not coming through with your part of the bargain and will let her down but I promised your mother we would be the first ones to drive the car we both worked so hard to purchase. I'm sure you understand this."

Note: Review the above as it triggers the template. First, the rephrasing of Hank's rebuttal in a caring fashion followed by Dad's decision. Remember this decision – you must repeat it as close to the original way it you said it as possible. Dad does not need to become upset or emotional as he has already "won the contest" and any emotional response added to his statement lessens the power of the template.

"Dad, don't you trust me?"

"Hank, I do trust you. You are without question mature enough to handle our new sports car. However, as I mentioned before, I promised your mother we would be the first ones to drive the car we both worked so hard to purchase. I'm sure you understand this."

Hank paused for a moment, then grinned and began again with both arms outstretched. "Wait a minute, I've got an idea. What if I picked her up in the car and we switch cars at the football game? That seems fair."

Still no emotion from Dad. He kept his tone steady. "I must give you credit for your clever thinking. Any other time this would probably work but I promised your mother we would be the first ones to drive the car we both worked so hard to purchase. I'm sure you understand this."

Hank grit his teeth and his face began to redden. "Well, if she drops me it's all your fault – I'll tell her so, too! Why are you being so unreasonable?"

"Hank, my good man, I would be very disappointed if Becky dropped you over a ride in the car but stranger things have happened, I'm sure. Please share with her the option I suggested of going out tomorrow. I know it may sound unreasonable but I promised your mother we would be the first ones to drive the car we both worked so hard to purchase. I'm sure you understand this."

Exasperated, Hank turned to the other side of the table. "Mom, can't you reason with Dad?"

She'd been quietly observing the entire conversation, fully aware of her husband's tactics. "Hank, your father and I discussed it and we agreed we would be the first ones to drive the car we both worked so hard to purchase. I'm sure you understand this."

"Fine, ruin my life, I hope you're happy!"

"To ruin your life would never make us happy," Mom continued, "but we agreed we would be the first ones to drive the car we both worked so hard to purchase. I'm sure you understand this."

Hank slowly pushed his chair back in, scratched his head, and looked back at his father. "Well, I've got to go call Becky and give her the bad news. I hope she'll understand," he shrugs. "You can't say I didn't give it my best try!"

"That you did. Good luck, Hank."

Hank headed for the door. "See ya."

Using the "broken record" template with MVP, Dad did not escalate Hank's emotion. Lucky for us, Mom knew about the “broken record” template and did not re-open the conversation, which can happen if not all parties are aware of the approach. Check this template out for yourself – did it work? Did you see how the decision was repeated as exactly as possible? Did you see how MVP allowed Dad to reflect Hank’s position with care, patience and full connection? Dad didn’t have to use his mental processing to create an answer to Hank’s responses as Dad already had his answer regardless of Hank’s rebuttal. Instead, Dad could use his energy, emotions and feelings to capture the full content and meaning of Hank’s responses and reflect them back. MVP at its best.

You can easily make the shift from a parent-to-child communication to an adult-to-adult communication style that fits well in the workplace. For example, a disagreement between a supervisor and a contentious employee who does not agree with an assignment or a contest between two employees in which one is demanding from the other one, irrationally. The applications are many for using MVP in conjunction with the “broken record” template.

Use MVP in concert with any leadership template.

Scenario #4: Preparing to Meet Your New Team for the First Time

As previously mentioned, MVP enhances any type of communication. One type of communication is presenting to a group of people. It can range from selling an idea, to coordinating a project team, to meeting your newly assigned team member.

As presented at the beginning of this chapter, it takes practice. Let's check in on Barbara, V.P. of Operations, as she prepares for her first meeting with her new management team generated from a recent merger. It was Barbara's first official day at this site, though she had been with the company for nearly two weeks. She spent the time in China at a corporate senior leadership strategic planning session – well worth her time, she felt.

Barb learned a lot about herself during the assessment process for this position. No surprises, but it gave her a better understanding of why she had evolved in her career and what new opportunities were there just for the taking.

Barbara's Profile:

- 46-year-old woman
- High "D" and "I"
- Mental Agility: 86th Percentile
- Vector/valence: -18.264; a no-nonsense, get-it-done type.
- Stress Quotient: 22; can handle stressful situations for longer periods than most before it affects her performance.
- Conflict Management: 52; a tough contender.
- Holds a Ph.D. in chemical engineering.
- Calls herself "seasoned," and even "spicy."
- Married to her career and wouldn't trade it for anything.

The first day of a new assignment was always a treat for her. This day would be no exception especially because she had just learned a new technique called MVP. She wanted to try it out and see if it worked as well as it had in class.

Team Profile:

- Five women, three men – each managing their own teams.

- Average age is 42 – youngest 24, oldest 59.
- Average years of service with company: 14.
- Average education level: Master's degree; all chemists.
- Combined vector/valence: -47.941; they would probably prefer to do their own thing.

Knowing all of this information, Barbara decided to use a servant-leader approach to lead and not manage the team. She had to be careful to stay on this path if she was to be effective.

The group's last leader accepted a "package" when the merger occurred. The position had been vacant for several months with the senior chemist "holding down the fort," as he liked to call it. He did not want the position because he planned to retire within the next couple of years. He was well liked and played a fatherly role.

Barbara paused and gazed out the window as she reflected on her MVP. The vision part came easily - she practiced visioning on a daily basis, so her focal length was well developed. Her vision was straightforward – these team members would choose her to be their leader over time and this first meeting would set this process in motion. The motivation falls in place behind the vision – simply gain the trust of this group. Lastly, her paradigm was that this is not a management team but her leadership partners. Her brief experience with MVP had yielded a trick – when you can't identify a motivation, move on to vision and then go back to motivation and paradigm. She was ready.

Barb's MVP:

M To gain the trust of her new team.

V This meeting would encourage the team members to choose her as their leader.

P Her team members are her leadership partners, not merely a management team.

Outside the door, she brushed off the sleeves of her jacket and smoothed her hair in place. With her shoulders square with confidence and a pleasant smile, she entered the conference room. "Good morning team. My name is Barbara Smith, my friends call me Barb, please call me Barb."

Barb went on. "Before we begin, let me say I'm humbled by being selected to be your senior partner. Having just had a chance to review your bio summaries I could not have asked for a more balanced, experienced and dedicated team. This team has all the right elements for us to be a standout division. I believe when we look back a couple of years from now we'll all be proud to add this experience to our résumés. I want each of our individual and professional reputations to grow significantly and to have fun while doing so.

“The uniqueness of this team would be a challenge for any manager. Therefore, I don’t plan to be your manager; I desire to be selected by you, each of you, as your leader. You’ll find me to be a pragmatist so I don’t have any misconceptions that you’ll give me this opportunity anytime soon – it is something I’m going to have to earn – decision by decision, conversation by conversation. It all starts with trust. Let’s take a few minutes and learn about our team. Does this work for you?”

The team absorbed Barb’s opening speech.

“Barb, what did you mean ‘we’d be a challenge?’?”

Barb looked across the table to the source of the question. The young woman was leaned back in her chair with her hands folded in her lap. “Jody, is it?”

“Yes, it is.”

Barb smiled. “Thanks for calling me ‘Barb’ and great question. Before I came here today, I looked at your profiles and added up the vector/valence of the group. The combined score is -47.941. My score is -18.264. You are more than double my score so to control you as a traditional manager would not work. However, to serve you as a leader would work, which is the approach I've selected to work with all of you. As you know, the closer the vector is to zero, the easier to manage."

Everyone's eyes darted around the room. "Barb, we never received our profiles or the scores. Will we ever get to see them?"

"Hmm, you need your results for us to work better together, I'm sorry that has yet to happen – we'll make that our first action item as a team. I'll schedule individual debriefings with each of you and then we'll meet to discuss what we learned that could help this team develop. Work for you?" Around the table, heads were nodding in agreement.

Barb took a marker from the table and stepped back to the pad of paper on an easel. "Now let's take a few minutes and learn something about each of us and our team. I would like each of you to tell me one value that you live by or drives you and your decision-making. Let's just go around the room and I'll put them on the flip chart. George, can we start with you?"

George straightened in his seat. "Yes… balance in all things, work-life included."

"Thank you," said Barb as she scribbled his answer. "Bob?"

"Health."

"Jody?"

"Integrity."

Barb paused before writing this one on the chart. "Interesting, what is your definition of 'integrity?'"

"Simply to do what you promise."

"Nice definition," she replied, adding the answer to the list. "Thank you. John?"

"Teamwork."

Barb tilted her head upward. "Tell me more."

"Well, teamwork is why we are together at the workplace. We can do more, think better ideas, and solve more problems as a team for starters."

"Thank you, I look forward to developing this more. Alice?"

"Respect for others."

"Good one, works for me. Karen?"

"Family."

"Sort of ties into 'balance,' doesn't it?" replied George, whose elbows were now propped on the table.

"It probably could, but let's keep it up there for now. Sandra?" continued Barb.

"I think mine is quality."

"Ok, Rebecca?"

"Family for me also."

Barb capped the marker and admired the finished list. "Thank you people, truly values we can use to develop our team." She went on, pointing to the chart, "I already see some themes that can weave a strong bond between us, but more about this later when we meet again.

"Although I don't want to take a lot of your time today, I just wanted to get started building the team. A couple administrative guidelines I will try to follow are that we will keep our staff meetings efficient but not to the level where we can't have creative and open conversation. Second, all of you are empowered to call a meeting of our team at any time to discuss or resolve an issue, address a problem or to coordinate our work. Don't wait for me. In all cases, I do not want to get in your way or slow progress. Any questions?"

The silence was deafening.

"By the way, team, my philosophy is 'silence is never consent or agreement.' What would you like to add before we go our different ways?"

"Barb, I'd like to thank John for being acting division head, he did a great job."

"Thanks for catching a very big error I just made. I think John deserves a standing ovation for holding the department together so well. If you will please join me as we all stand and applaud John." Without hesitation, the group stood in applause and whistled for the efforts of their team member. John raised his hand in modesty and kept his eyes on the table, though he couldn't hide his smile.

Barbara was beaming. "This is an awesome team, I can see it already. Thank you all and I'll get you set up to go over your profiles. Have a good day."

Take some time to review this staff meeting. What did Barb do right? Did her MVP seep through her staff meeting? Do you feel there is any chance her vision to become their leader will become reality? Would you move towards following her? Her motivation to gain their trust – did admitting her mistake move her toward gaining their trust? Could you see her paradigm of "leadership partners" start to emerge?

As many successful people will attest, you can become what you think. MVP is the form or vessel you should use to contain the content of any discussion.

You can become what you think.

Scenario #5: Mentoring

Let's go back to the first scenario about Brad's relationship with his new boss, Pam. Remember his vision of Pam becoming his mentor? Let's see how they're doing.

It's been two months since Pam began as Branch manager. Brad has been everything he promised her the first day they met to discuss the Limekey project. He kept his team on track and they seemed to enjoy his leadership.

In fact, deep down she wished they would see her more as their leader as they did Brad. But it was early yet; she had plenty of time to win her following.

However, Dale was getting under her skin. He ran support services, facilities, publications, IT services and even field support. He was like an office manager on steroids. He was a former Marine – precise and squared away, as others labeled him.

Dale's Profile:

- 51 year-old man
- High "D"
- Mental Agility: 87th Percentile
- Vector/valence: -42.760; intense, "get it done and then we can take a break" mentality.
- Stress Quotient: 26; he would often joke that if it was getting too hot in the kitchen, he would turn up the heat – it "separated the men from the boys."
- Often brags that his team never missed a deadline.
- Recently married for the 2nd time; speaks with great respect of his new wife.
- Has two grown children from his prior marriage.

Pam just about had enough. "Brad, do you have time for lunch tomorrow? I need some mentoring." Pam caught Brad off guard.

"Well, ah, sure any particular topic?"

"It's Dale, I'll tell you all about it tomorrow at lunch."

"I look forward to it, see you then."

The next day at twelve o'clock sharp, Pam was knocking at Brad's office door. After a very fast ride in Pam's sporty sedan, they sat down at a local Italian restaurant – a company favorite. Brad and Pam each ordered salads with iced teas.

After they had placed their order, Brad initiated the topic. His MVP was well in place – Motivation, to be of real value to Pam; Vision, to help Pam have her issue addressed so successfully she'd be encouraged to seek out further mentoring from Brad; and the Paradigm was Pam was a quick study who made mentoring a pleasure.

Brad's MVP:

M To be of real value to his mentor, Pam.

V Pam's issue would be addressed so successfully that she'd be encouraged to seek further mentoring from him.

P Pam is a quick study who would make mentoring a pleasure.

"Please, tell me about Dale." It was a simple request. He did not want to appear too expert by asking how he could help her. He wasn't even sure how much she really wanted his help.

"If you hadn't earned my trust over the last couple months I wouldn't have come to you. I need your help. Dale is becoming my worst nightmare. He is everything I can't handle in an employee. Every time I work with him he erodes my self esteem as a manager."

Brad leaned forward and looked steadily at Pam. Her eyes were moist and neither noticed their salads had already arrived.

Brad softened his voice. "This sounds serious; I've got your back so lay it out for me."

"Well, Dale is so confident and sure of himself all the time that when I say something to one of his people – even an idea – they look to him to get his approval. I'm his boss! He makes me feel like his child or new supervisor and he's the expert. I don't feel he respects me, needs my input, or advice let alone take direction from me," with a quick breath, she went on, "I've never had to pull rank before but maybe that's what I'm going to have to do to get his attention." She paused. "Make him stand at attention when I talk to him." She stabbed a chunk of lettuce with her fork.

"Seems he has you royally upset," Brad offered.

"You grasp the obvious well!" When Brad sat back, offended, she apologized. "I'm sorry to be so sharp, but I've just had it."

Brad sighed. "I've been there myself, Pam, and not that long ago."

"You, mister cool leader?"

"I'll take that as a compliment but that has only come recently."

"Really? How'd you do it?"

"It all started with Leadership Flight School™. They were introducing the concept of the servant leader. Wow, what a shift of paradigm for me. The model I had been using was the manager model, based in control. You have to be able to control your people in whatever way possible – manipulation, intimidation, fear, withhold rewards; oh, the list just goes on and on. I was quite expert in using a wide range of these control techniques. I knew someday I'd meet someone who was an excellent performer but that I couldn't control. Sounds like you just met this person."

Pam was leaning forward, slowing chewing as Brad spoke. With a gulp she said, "I never thought of it that way but it does seem to describe my situation with Dale. Tell me more."

"Well, when you put yourself in a position to serve your subordinates instead of being on top controlling them, your paradigm shifts. You encourage them to unleash their potential – the better they become technically, as leaders and as contributors, the more you should celebrate their progress and success. It reflects back on you. It is not a competition for you to be better than they are. Your job is to help them become all they can be. You need to be proud of having a team that excels beyond your abilities. You have already arrived or you would not have your current position. Now your job is to prepare them to have your job so you are free to move further up the ladder of success."

"That is quite a paradigm shift for me – I'll have to chew on that for awhile to really get it." Pushing her salad away and leaning forward, she almost whispered, "Where do I start?"

"MVP."

"Sounds like a medicine."

"It's actually better than medicine. It stands for three elements you must have clearly in your mind before you talk to Dale. The 'M' stands for the motivation for your conversation, the 'V' stands for your vision of the outcome of the conversation and the 'P' is your paradigm or lens you are looking through to translate the conversation you are about to have. The most critical piece is that all of these three elements must be positive. If they are not, don't start the conversation. My personal experience is this really works." Brad's "MVP man" was very pleased at this point.

"Sounds like hard work, how long did it take you to learn to do this?"

"Just take it one conversation at a time, it will grow on you as you become more and more successful in your conversations. They will see you are truly trying to serve them."

"Positive about Dale, that is a tall order. What would your MVP be with Dale given what I've told you?"

Brad took a long sip of his iced tea, giving him time to think. As he set his glass down, he replied, "Let's do a negative MVP first as this will come naturally and will allow you to see the drastic difference when you create a positive MVP."

"Ok, I can do that! My motivation would be to knock him down a few pegs, my vision would be to have him lose some of his ego and cocky self-confidence and have to rely on me, and the paradigm is he is a necessary evil I must deal with." Pam stopped to reflect on what she had just said. "I bet I come across as a real head case to you."

"Actually, no," he assured her. "You just feel intense. You really captured a negative MVP. Now let's attempt a positive MVP."

"Ok, ah… my motivation is to hear Dale and select the positive suggestions he offers to leverage them to get the job done," Pam spoke slowly and deliberately, thinking through each word. "My vision is I appreciate his contributions and my paradigm is we are not competitors but collaborators." Pam looked at Brad, whose mouth hung slightly open. "Well…?"

"Pam, that is fantastic – that is why you are on the way to become our COO. You learn extremely fast, are bluntly honest with your feelings and sincerely take the risks to develop yourself. I'm proud to know you. Go for it."

Pam beamed. "Thank you Brad, once again I owe you."

"Nope, just let me know how it works out for you. It's an honor to work with you."

Back at work, Pam put her newfound MVP skills to the test. Within three months, Dale insisted that Pam meet his wife and he cooked for both of them, a skill no one knew he had.

It should be apparent how MVP can be a life-changing and career-saving tool. What would have happened if Pam had "pulled rank" on Dale? Would both of them still be working together? Maybe, but maybe they would have been even worse off than before.

Scenario #6: Stranger to Stranger

Lisa forced her bulging bag into the overhead compartment – she finally made it. Things were coming together. She had an aisle seat and she was the first to arrive in her three-seat row. Maybe, just maybe, it wouldn't be a full flight and she could spread out with her pillow and blanket and get some much-needed sleep. She had been up late the night before saying goodbye to her new friends she made at Leadership Flight School™. She was gone a week but it seemed like only yesterday she was traveling to the leadership course. *What a life-changing experience… but back to the grindstone.* An elderly man interrupted her drifting thoughts with, "I'm by the window." He placed his worn leather briefcase in the overhead and took his seat with newspaper in hand.

Still, she might win the lottery of no-one-sitting-in-the-middle-seat. She settled back into her comfortable pose. No point in fastening the seatbelt yet because it would only bring bad luck of someone sitting in the middle seat. She wasn't superstitious, but why tempt fate anyway? It's like carrying an umbrella to keep rain away.

The older gentleman had already fallen asleep and it looked like they were closing the cabin door – almost there.

Glancing around, Lisa noticed it was a full flight after all. The flight attendant reopened the door to one more passenger – *my luck*, Lisa reflected. Coming down the aisle with two shopping bags came a large glistening – no, sweating – woman. Her shopping bags managed to make contact with each person on the aisle as she shuffled through with the appropriate, "excuse me," "pardon me," and "can I get by?" statements.

She stopped next to Lisa and looked down over her glasses. "I'm there," pointing to the empty seat next to Lisa.

A belt extender would be required for sure, Lisa surmised, as she made peace with herself that she not only lost her comfort but now was sharing her part of the seat as well. As she wedged herself back into her seat, she wondered if they made seat horns like they made shoehorns. Anyway, if they did there was never one around when you needed it.

Maybe it was because she was tired that she felt her negative emotions start to warm up, or maybe it was simply because this woman was violating her space. There was no more room in the overhead compartments to place her shopping bags so one was under the woman's feet and one, "I hope you don't mind," under Lisa's feet.

Normally Lisa was more forgiving of other passengers, but this woman looked like she just crawled out of bed, her hair uncombed, disheveled clothing, and no make-up, the whole works – or lack thereof.

The woman started, "I thought I was going to miss the plane – I got here just in time."

Lisa had a decision to make – connect with this woman and possibly have to endure talking to her part or most of the trip, or to ignore the woman, hoping she would get the hint and leave her alone.

Funny, Lisa had just come from a leadership program where one of the tools they had to use was MVP before they could have conversations. She had rather enjoyed the technique and had hoped she could practice it sometime soon, but she wasn't expecting this soon. *Well, why not put it to the test – probably the worst case she would meet in quite awhile.*

Well, there was the motivation, maybe to keep her mind off being squeezed to death. No, that was a bit too negative; it had to be positive. Well, how about getting to know her at a deeper level? Her father had told her you couldn't hate someone when you know something about him or her or some such saying. Her vision would be to enjoy the trip in spite of the cozy conditions. Now the hard part – a positive paradigm. Well, she was a fellow passenger, wasn't that enough? It would have to do for now.

Lisa's MVP:

M To get to know this woman at a deeper level.

V To have an enjoyable flight.

P This woman is a fellow passenger.

Lisa probed into the woman's comment. "Did you get tied up in traffic?" A bit of a sarcastic question since it was 6 a.m. and traffic would have been minimal.

"Oh, no," responded the woman, "I got a phone call at three o'clock this morning from my friend. She was calling from the hospital because her husband had a serious farming accident and had just gotten out of emergency surgery. He's in critical condition," the woman continued to open up to Lisa. "They have five children under 10 and live out in the country where they farm. My dear friend was beside herself saying she didn't know what she was going to do. I told her I'd take the next plane out. Here I am, a mess."

Overwhelmed, Lisa's paradigm snapped into its positive place. This woman wasn't a mess; she was selfless, without caring for herself or her dignity – it was all about someone else. Lisa scolded herself – when would she stop judging the book by the cover? She needed this lesson. She extended her hand, "I'm Lisa, and sounds like you have your work waiting for you."

"I'm Betsy, nice to have someone to talk to. Yes, it could be a challenge but I couldn't let my friend down." She finished by wiping her brow with a damp napkin.

"Where does your friend live?"

"South of Des Moines, close to Stanzel."

"Isn't that near the covered bridges of the famous Madison County?" Lisa asked.

"Well, not far as I'm told. They recently bought the small farm and I haven't been there to see it yet."

"Well, you'll get a good look now."

Betsy sighed. "I think you're right. Where do you live, Lisa, near there?"

"Not too far, I live north of Des Moines, near Ames." It was Lisa's turn to help someone. "Betsy, how are you getting to the farm?"

After a long pause, Betsy, speaking carefully and thoughtfully, responded. "I really never thought of it in all my rush. Do the taxis go that far?"

"I don't really know, but don't worry about it. I'll take you there."

"Oh, I can't ask you to do that, but that would be a real blessing."

"Please allow me to contribute a little to you and your situation. I have the whole day off anyway."

"Well, if it isn't too much trouble..."

"No problem, then it's settled."

"Yes, I'll call my friend when we land and let her know she doesn't need to worry about me getting to her home."

By the end of the flight, Betsy and Lisa had become fast friends. Lisa actually worked that day on the farm, and helped Betsy settle in with her "new temporary family."

MVP is not complex, nor does it take a long time to activate, but it has a powerful influence over the success of your communications and relationships, in and outside the workplace.

Scenario #7: The Interview

Fred Johnson sat in his favorite chair by the big bay window and stared across his property to the farmer tilling the field in the distance. Three weeks ago, the 49-year-old lost his job at a printing company after 21 years of service. His shop closed abruptly after a competitor purchased the business. He received one week of pay for each year of service, nearly a half of a year of severance. He had a BS and MBA, married with three children. One is a sophomore in college, one age 17 and one age 15, and both college-bound. His wife Joanne was a secretary in their local municipal office.

Only a slight problem. He lived in a rather rural area where the largest town was an hour and fifteen minute's drive away, so jobs were limited. His parents were getting older and lived 20 minutes away. His wife's parents were much older and were on assisted living across town, so his wife was opposed to relocating. His two youngest sons were outstanding athletes in the local high school; if they continued their successes, they could both get scholarships to college.

Deep down he knew his plant supervision days were over. He knew he had to work to finish his home mortgage, two car payments, college tuition for his kids and maintain his family health insurance. Life was looking rather grim. He didn't have the money or time to go back to school. He had worked 55 to 60 hours every week for years. He was uncomfortable just sitting around looking at the want ads. He did find one job right away, but within the first week, his new boss wanted to move him to their El Paso plant. Fred rejected the offer and was let go.

A friend put him in touch with a career counselor. After a day of testing and coaching, he decided to apply for an Assistant Superintendent position at the local youth detention facility. He had always liked working with the Boy Scouts and his church youth group. This might be the career shift he needed. He would have no problem working 15 or more years and best of all, it was a seven-minute drive from his home. The money was about 20% less but the benefits were actually better. He could do some painting jobs in the evenings and on weekends and it could come out to a positive cash flow.

He was elated – the counselor sure was worth what he charged! One hurdle left – the interview. He found out that seven others were also up for consideration. Three already worked there, one was a licensed psychologist, and three he knew nothing about. Tough competition in tough times. He had to land this job. He went back to the career counselor for more help.

Dr. Bill greeted him warmly and congratulated him on his career choice. He then got down to business.

"Fred, how can I help you?"

Fred outlined his interest in the job and his concerns about the competition, specifically the fact he had not had a true interview in 21 years.

"Well, let's start at the beginning," suggested Bill. "It all begins with your MVP."

"My what?" asked Fred.

"Your motivation, vision and paradigm about your interview. It all has to be positive if you want to optimize your chances of having a successful interview."

"Tell me more," Fred said as he scratched the back of his neck.

"Your motivation should be other-centered, focused on the company or organization for which you are interviewing. How you can serve and make a significant contribution to the organization. In other words, how you would add to the success of your future employer. Your answers will then reflect a deep respect for the position and the employer. It's never about you, even when they ask a question about you."

Fred took it all in. He had his family to think about. "That's different but I can understand your point. I would have done that wrong for sure. Please go on," said Fred.

"Second is your vision or the 'V' component of the MVP. Your vision is the process of looking longer term at the outcome of the interview, or even the results of any communication you encounter."

Fred understood immediately. “It’s sort of like imagining the outcome of the interview, like they see you as someone they would like to have work with them?”

“You have it, Fred. Let’s move to the ‘P’ or paradigm. The ‘P’ is the mindset or lens you are looking through about the position. If its negative, it’ll be felt by the interviewer because they are looking at all clues, verbal and non-verbal, that tell your story and who you are as a person.”

Fred thought for a moment. He readjusted his seated position in the stiff armchair and asked, “I’m not getting this. Could you give me an example?”

“Sure, a positive paradigm could be simply that this job is not a job, but a career that will challenge you up through retirement.”

“Oh, I see it now – the paradigm shift is from a job to a career. I got it!”

Fred found the session with Dr. Bill to be very helpful. They covered many aspects of interviewing, all starting with MVP. Fred role-played the interview numerous times, each one beginning with a different MVP. Fred was ready – bring it on!

Fred's MVP:

M To add to the success of the potential employer.

V The employer will want Fred to work for them.

P This would be a new career, not just a job.

Fred went home and continued to practice. When it came time for interview, he felt confident in himself and his potential career. Fred had a second interview, and then they made him an offer. Fred continued working as the Assistant Superintendent for fourteen years before he retired and continued service as a volunteer for the facility.

10

Go!

You are now ready to run the race. Ready, set, go! MVP has many characteristics of a race. The M, or motivation, gives you the reason you are running the race. The V, or vision, gives you the ideal destination or positive outcome for the race. The P, or paradigm, gives you your direction.

The rewards of having better relationships and wonderful conversations will keep you going. It does not require the level of self-control required by a diet or the dedication of breaking a bad habit. You can forget to do it, even for several days, and it will continue to develop with your next usage. It does not lose its strength with intermittent use. However, the more it is used the more predictable the results.

The fascinating experience many users report is that not only do they become happier with their relationships, but they also feel better about themselves. Just sitting down with their breakfast coffee and envisioning the conversations they already know they will be having from an MVP perspective gives a positive start for the day.

Some users suggest it even addresses mild depression. Dread of the day or fear of the unknown disappears; it's our relationships that challenge us. Preparing our positive MVP gives us a better chance for us to have a successful day.

For MVP to work, you do not need to prepare it right before the communication event. It can be prepared hours and in some cases days ahead and still yield good results. Once your MVP is firmly placed in your mind it can be easily recalled when the event occurs.

Most people desire to help others. Deep down, they at least wish to serve others, even if it is for a fleeting moment. From a nice word, to a smile, to a pleasant impromptu conversation on a park bench, to a serious discussion on some interesting topic, all conversations should start with MVP. Make your life and the lives of others richer with the giving of yourself. It doesn't require dollars, disruption of your daily routine, or even require you to go to a foreign land to provide to others. Using your MVP is a gift that will keep on giving. It is your decision – no one else's – to let go of your reservations about this tool and try it.

Many years ago, Dale Carnegie wrote a well received and respected book called, "How to Win Friends and Influence

People." MVP will help you accomplish just that – to win friends and influence people.

Now that you have read the book, please pass it on. Discuss the results of your MVP journey with others. Share techniques, create a list of motivations you hear about, constantly work on refining your visions and have fun hearing about unique paradigms.

Keep a journal of your successes and those few fumbles that will inevitably occur. You can learn from both. This journal will allow you to create your own ending to this book. May your ending be to your satisfaction. Do well!

Additional Information

Understanding yourself and others can help you get the most out of the MVP template. Through assessment technologies, you can learn more by measuring:

- DISCription Temperament Inventory
- Vector/Valence
- Stress Quotient
- Mental Agility
- Workplace Stress
- Conflict Management
- And more!

For more information on MVP, assessments and other tools, please contact us or visit us on the web:

Bartell & Bartell, Ltd.
432 Rolling Ridge Drive, Suite 4
State College, PA 16801
(814) 861-6606
www.bartellbartell.com
info@bartellbartell.com